THE TRIVIA CHALLENGE

300 FUN QUESTIONS AND FACTS FOR KIDS AND FAMILY

Riddleland

Designs by Freepik.com

Table of Contents

Table of Contents

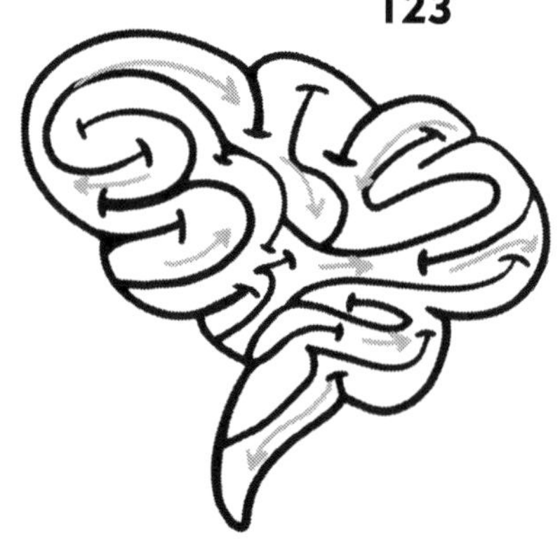

Introduction

"What we learn with pleasure, we never forget." ~ Alfred Mercier

Research has shown that trivia has positive effects on the brain. Aside from offering young minds a way to pass the time, trivia books bolster confidence, offer a fun way of learning, and foster the critical thinking skills that will benefit a child for life.

Whether you're hosting a children's party or going on a long road trip, trivia questions are also the perfect way to engage children while building interpersonal relationships. Question and answer sessions create an exchange between participants that has been shown to boost dopamine levels in the brain. Thereby, creating feelings of positivity and togetherness that will far outlast the game.

Throughout our book, we have created unique questions that will both challenge and entertain your child. While some of the answers are easy to guess, others will require deductive reasoning and logic skills. No matter the case, each question and answer series offers facts and names that any curious mind will want to research further.

Our questions are chock full of facts and figures that children will remember for years to come. Once they learn about places, people, and things in trivia form, they are likely to recall the answers more easily than if they were simply read out of a textbook.

Pay careful attention to the way questions are worded and the answer possibilities. There are small clues hidden within each one. Keep score as you go along, and remember to see all incorrect answers as learning opportunities rather than something wrong. Most importantly, remember to have fun!

https://pixelfy.me/riddlelandbonus

Thank you for buying this book. We would like to share a special bonus as a token of appreciation. It is a collection of 50 original jokes, riddles, and two funny stories

LAND ANIMALS

LOOK DEEP INTO NATURE AND THEN YOU WILL UNDERSTAND EVERYTHING
~ NATURE'S QUOTE

HOW MUCH DO YOU KNOW ABOUT THINGS THAT CREEP, CRAWL, AND FLY?

1. Do you know which one of these animals belongs to the reptile family?
a) Grizzly bear
b) Turtle
c) Peacock
d) Chinchilla

2. Can you figure out which one of these Arctic animals is sometimes called the skunk bear because of its black and white markings?
a) Wolverine
b) Polar bear
c) Caribou
d) Moose

3. Which one of these big, scary animals can go for six months without food?
a) Ostrich
b) Elephant
c) Crocodile
d) Koala

4. Which one of these animals goes into hibernation every fall and returns in the spring?
a) Groundhog
b) Bluejay
c) Tiger
d) Red fox

5. There are more of this bird than there are people; can you guess which one?
a) Pigeon
b) Crow
c) Starling
d) Chicken

6. What part of the anteater would you say is the longest?
a) Legs
b) Tail
c) Tongue
d) Nose

7. What kind of noisy monkey lives in the jungles of Central and South America?
a) Screeching monkey
b) Laughing monkey
c) Howler monkey
d) Complaining monkey

8. Most cats don't like to swim — what's the name of the one that does?

a) Lynx
b) Leopard
c) Jaguar
d) Lion

---

9. Which part of a dog's body sweats the most?

a) Forehead
b) Back
c) Tail
d) Paws

---

10. Which one of these animals is North America's biggest tree-eating rodent?

a) Beaver
b) Deer mouse
c) Prairie dog
d) Vole

---

11. Can you guess which one of these farm animals chews something called a cud?

a) Horse
b) Goat
c) Rooster
d) Cow

12. What's the name of the colorful bird that you sometimes see sitting on a pirate's shoulder?

a) Sparrow
b)Raven
c) Whippoorwill
d) Parrot

13. Can you correctly pick the animal that is NOT a mammal from this list?

a) Skink
b)Cheetah
c) Chimpanzee
d) Hedgehog

14. What's the name of the huge, horse-like animal you might see in the woods of Alaska or Canada?

a) Moose
b) Jack rabbit
c) Ocelot
d) Canary

15. Do you know which one of these animals is also called the American buffalo?

a) Mule deer
b) Nutria
c) Bison
d) Emu

16. Can you guess which part of a squirrel never stops growing?

a) Teeth
b) Tail
c) Paws
d) Brain

17. Do you know which one of these furry animals is a distant relative of the camel?

a) Coyote
b)Llama.
c) Hedgehog
d) Zebra

18. Which one of these animals might do a little warning dance before spraying you with smelly stuff?

a) Llama
b) Skunk
c) Lemur
d) Sloth

19. What's the name of the snake that can puff out a hood when it's agitated?

a) King cobra
b) Garter snake
c) Black mamba
d) Ball python

20. Since rabbits are herbivores, what food would they never eat?
a) Cheeseburger b) Lettuce
c) Wheat d) Cabbage

21. Do you know which mammal is the only mammal that can fly?
a) Walrus b) Pig
c) Bat d) Dolphin

22. Which one of these animals has hooves that shrink in the wintertime?
a) Mallard duck b) Sloth
c) Reindeer d) Cougar

23. Out of these flying insects, which one will not bite you?
a) Flea b)Mosquito
c) Bumblebee d) Dragonfly

24. When people talk about their long, short Dachshund dogs, what nickname do they sometimes use?
a) Sausage dog b) Hamburger dog
c) Bacon dog d) Chicken dog

25. Which of these animals has a bill like a duck and lives in Australia and Tasmania?
a) Kangaroo b) Platypus
c) Whooping crane d) Alligator

26. Can you choose the dog breed that always has curly hair?
a) Poodle b) Pug
c) Chihuahua d) Labrador retriever

27. What important sounding name is given to the tallest kind of penguin?

a) Boss penguin
b) Parent penguin
c) President penguin
d) Emperor penguin

---

28. Do you know which one of these nocturnal animals can rotate its head 270 degrees?

a) Raccoon
b) Tasmanian devil
c) Skunk
d) Owl

---

29. On a farm, they are called pigs; what are the wild version with tusks called?

a) Boars
b) Elephants
c) Ponies
d) Muskrats

---

30. Which of these names is the right name for a group of toads?

a) Gang
b) Knot
c) Pride
d) School

ANSWER

1. b) Turtle.
Along with snakes, crocodiles, and lizards, turtles are reptiles. Unlike mammals, reptiles cannot regulate their own body heat and have to use their environments to stay warm.

2. a) Wolverine.
Wolverines are the biggest members of the weasel family, and they love to eat. In fact, they like food so much that they have been known to fight polar bears for it!

3. c) Crocodile.
Both saltwater and freshwater crocodiles have been known to eat only twice a year. When a food source gets low, they often stick around until there's something else to eat.

4. a) Groundhog.
Even though there's a day in February named after groundhogs, they don't come up to see their shadow until spring. Groundhogs, sometimes called woodchucks, are the biggest animal in the squirrel family.

5. d) Chicken.
With 25 billion of them in the world, there are over three times more chickens than there are humans. A female chicken can lay over 300 eggs every year, so it's easy to see why there are so many of them!

6. c) Tongue.
Whether you're talking about a kitten-sized or the giant-sized anteater, its tongue is always the longest part of its body. Anteaters use their long tongues to reach way down inside anthills and other insect nests.

7. c) Howler monkey.
All kinds of monkeys can make noises, but howler monkeys are the loudest. Their mighty howl can be heard from five miles away!

8. c) Jaguar.
Behind lions and tigers, jaguars are the third biggest of all the big cats. They tend to live near rivers and lakes, and they have no problem taking a swim to find food.

9. d) Paws.
Even though every single one of a dog's hair follicles has a tiny sweat gland, dogs only sweat through the parts without fur. You can find dog sweat on their noses and their paws.

10. a) Beaver.
Beavers are easily recognized by their big front teeth and their paddle-like tail. Although they will occasionally eat leafy plants, they mostly prefer to munch on the trees that grow near rivers and lakes.

11. d) Cow.
For over seven hours a day, cows chew on a wad of regurgitated food called a cud that comes from one of its four digestive chambers. Cows are vegetarians, and they only like to eat grasses, wheat, and oats.

12. d) Parrot.
Across tropical regions, there are over 370 different species of parrots. Only a few of them can mimic the human voice and ask for things like crackers

13. a) Skink.
Skinks are lizards, and lizards are reptiles. All the other animals are mammals because they are warm-blooded and covered in fur, and they produce milk.

14. a) Moose.
Moose can grow up to 7.5 feet tall. Although they might look a little like a horse with giant antlers, they are a member of the deer family.

15. c) Bison.
Bison can weigh up to 2,000 pounds and run up to 40 miles per hour! They are prehistoric creatures that once roamed the plains alongside wooly mammoths.

16. a) Teeth.
If you were to see a squirrel chewing on something, there's a very good reason for it. Since their teeth never stop growing, they have to gnaw on things to keep them the perfect size.

17. b) Llama.
Llamas don't have humps, but they are part of the camel family. Just like their bigger cousins, llamas have three stomachs and eat a vegetarian diet.

18. b) Skunk.
Skunks might be cute, but they can leave a bad smell anywhere they feel threatened. Their white stripes point toward their scent gland, which they use to keep predators away.

19. a) King cobra.
King cobras are considered one of the world's most deadly snakes. Measuring up to 12 feet long, they are also one of the longest.

20. a) Cheeseburger.
There are over 300 different types of rabbits, and none of them eat meat. You would never find one eating a cheeseburger, but they have been known to invade a cabbage patch or two.

21. c) Bat.
Many people think that bats are blind, but it's not true. Bats find insects to eat using both special night time vision and echolocation.

22. c) Reindeer.
Reindeers have a couple of abilities that help them survive in the wild. Their hooves expand and contract with the weather, and their noses heat up cold air before it goes into their bodies.

23. d) Dragonfly.
Dragonflies have been traced back almost 300 million years, and they've never been known to bite. When dragonflies are born, they spend up to 12 months living in the water.

24. a) Sausage dog.
Originally created to chase rats out of tunnels, Dachshunds are also called weiner dogs. Their elongated bodies make them look a little like a sausage.

25. b) Platypus.
The platypus is a furry mammal with a duck's nose and webbed feet. They use the cells on their bills to avoid predators by sensing them before they see them.

26. a) Poodle.
There are three types of poodles. The standard poodle can measure up to two feet tall, and the miniature version barely reaches a foot.

27. d) Emperor penguin.
There are 17 different types of penguins, and the Emperor penguin is almost as big as you are. They can stand up to 48 inches tall!

28. d) Owl.
Owls are able to move their heads so far because their necks can bend 135 degrees in either direction. Their eyes don't move like ours do, so being able to turn their head is very important.

29. a) Boars.
Around the farm, pigs are intelligent creatures that can learn their names within two days of being born. In the wild, they are called boars, and they are dangerous creatures.

30. b) Knot.
If you found a group of toads in your backyard, you have found a knot. You would never find a knot in Antarctica, though. Toads have never been found there.

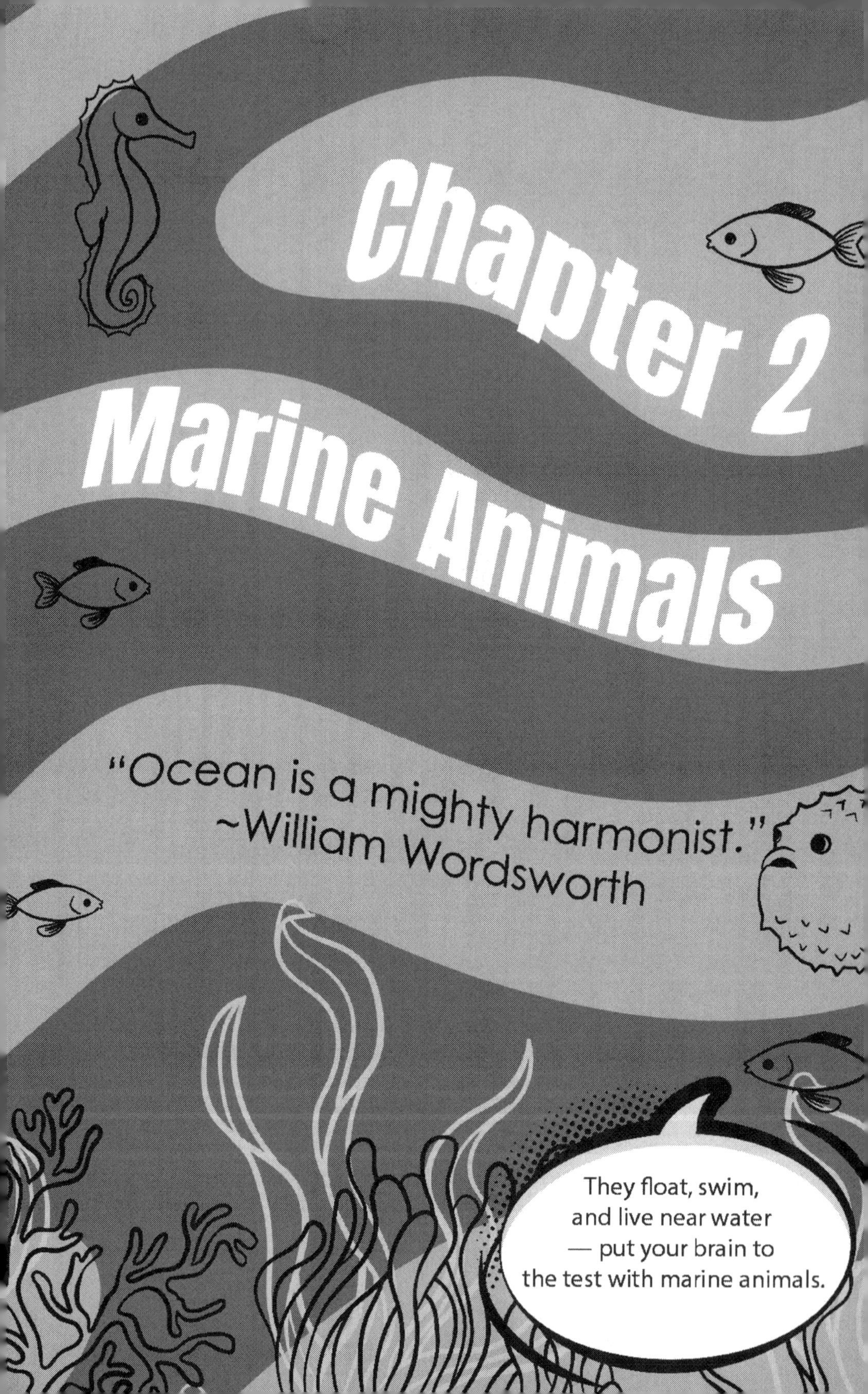

Chapter 2
Marine Animals
"Ocean is a mighty harmonist."
~William Wordsworth
They float, swim, and live near water — put your brain to the test with marine animals.

1. What part of their bodies do jellyfish use to sting and paralyze their prey?

a) Tentacles
b) Hood
c) Stomach pouch
d) Mouth

2. Do you know which one of these shelled animals has no idea when to quit growing?

a) Lobster
b) Hermit crab
c) Giant squid
d) Manta ray

3. Which one of these things would you never find in a shark's body?

a) Bones
b) Muscles
c) Gills
d) Stomach

4. What do you think that sea snakes like to eat most?

a) Fish
b) Sponges
c) Octopus
d) Stingrays

5. What's the name of the ocean creature that has five arms and sand dollars for cousins?

a) Sea urchin
b) Vaquita
c) Electric eel
d) Starfish

6. Which big marine mammal is the cousin of the dugong and sometimes called the elephant of the sea?

a) Otter
b) Walrus
c) Manatee
d) Polar bear

7. You might find a pearl if you crack open which animal's shell?

a) Lobster
b) Crab
c) Tortoise
d) Oyster

8. Can you figure out which kind of bear is classified as a marine animal?

a) Panda bear
b) Polar bear
c) Brown bear
d) Sun bear

9. What part of a walrus' body can grow up to three feet long?

a) Whiskers
b) Tusks
c) Nose
d) Hair

10. What ocean bird has a giant pouch attached to its beak?

a) Pelican
b) Seagull
c) Raven
d) Crane

11. What funny-sounding fish is known for its orange, white and black stripes?

a) Flounder
b) Clownfish
c) Jumping mullet
d) Pinfish

12. Do you know which one of these seal names is a real name?

a) Noseless seal
b) Eyeless seal
c) Earless seal
d) Whiskerless seal

13. What kind of marine animal do you think a gag grouper might be?

a) Anemone
b) Eel
c) Fish
d) Seal

14. What's the name of the animal that has long really tentacles and eyeballs the size of a dinner plate?

a) Blue whale
b) Manatee
c) Giant squid
d) Porpoise

15. Which farm animal's name is sometimes used when talking about a female whale?

a) Goat
b) Chicken
c) Cow
d) Horse

16. Which type of underwater animal can shock its prey and predators with 600 volts?

a) Electric eel
b) Nurse shark
c) Orca
d) Sea snail

17. Do you know which one of these animals is a relative of the shark?

a) Stingray
b) Seagull
c) Axolotl
d) Seahorse

18. What's the name of the marine animal that can confuse its prey by shooting ink?

a) Squid
b) Coral
c) Stingray
d) Vaquita

19. Which one of these poisonous fish might you mistake for a rock?

a) Pufferfish
b) Stonefish
c) Yellow tang
d) Triggerfish

20. Can you figure out the name of the shy crab that likes to use seashells for a home?

a) Coconut crab
b) Hermit crab
c) Alaskan king crab
d) Japanese spider crab

21. What ocean fish communicates using a language of clicks and whistles?

a) Tuna
b)Marlin
c) Dolphin
d) Goblin shark

22. Which one of these barrier animals barely moves and forms reefs?

a) Coral
b) Jellyfish
c) Oyster
d) Angelfish

23. Do you know which of these sea creatures likes to travel in pairs joined by their curly tails?

a) Mako sharks
b) Sea otters
c) Seahorses
d) Squid

24. Which one of these absolutely huge animals doesn't have any teeth?

a) Lamprey
b) Moray eel
c) Plankton
d) Humpback whale

25. Unless it's prepared by a really smart chef, which one of these balloon-like fish is poisonous to humans?

a) Ahi tuna
b) Pufferfish
c) Sea urchin
d) Sardine

26. How do you think sea lions make their way across stretches of land?

a) They do belly flops
b) They walk
c) They roll
d) They fly

27. The lamprey has 11 or 12 frightening rows of which body part?

a) Eyes
b) Teeth
c) Nostrils
d) Claws

28. What animal belongs in the spineless group of creatures called invertebrates?

a) Dolphin
b) Whale
c) Shrimp
d) Albatross

29. We call it a triggerfish, but what do they call it in Hawaii?

a) Humuhumunukunukuapua'a
b) Lionfish
c) Hulafish
d) Volcanofish

30. Which one of these things do octopuses not like to do?

a) Swim
b) Hang out with other octopuses
c) Hide
d) Climb rocks

ANSWER

1. a) Tentacles.
When jellyfish get hungry, they use small cells on their tentacles to paralyze food before putting it into their mouths. Jellyfish also use their mouths to go to the bathroom.

2. a) Lobster.
Lobsters and cucumbers are the only things on the planet that don't know when to stop growing. Since they can live up to 100 years, they can grow to weigh 40 pounds!

3. a) Bones.
If you were to x-ray a shark, you wouldn't find any bones. Instead, they have cartilage like the flexible, tough stuff that makes up your nose and your ears.

4. a) Fish.
Most kinds of sea snakes love to eat fish, but a couple of them prefer fish eggs instead. Sea snakes are poisonous, but their fangs never grow big enough to bite through wetsuits.

5. a) Starfish.
There are over 2,000 different varieties of starfish, and they always have five arms, sometimes more. If they lose an arm, they simply grow it back through a process called regeneration.

6. c) Manatee.
Both manatees and dugongs belong to a family of marine mammals called sirenians. With only 10,000 dugongs left in the world, it's important to protect them.

7. d) Oyster.
Pearls are formed when oysters surround a piece of sand with special liquids that stop scratching or irritation.

8. a) Polar bear.
Polar bears are considered marine animals because they can live quite happily on the ice of the Arctic Ocean. They also spend a lot of time in the water trying to catch their favorite snack — seals.

9. b) Tusks.
Walruses use their giant tusks for more than just hunting. The longer their tusks grow, the higher they sit in the walrus social ladder.

10. a) Pelican.
Many people think that pelicans keep their food in the pouch attached to their beak. They actually use it to catch the day's meal by swooping it out of the water, but they never store it there.

11. b) Clownfish.
If you close your eyes and picture Nemo, you are picturing a clownfish. There are over 20 types of them, and they love living in coral reefs.

12. c) Earless seal.
Also called true seals, earless seals are born without the pinnae needed for ears to form. Even without them, they have remarkably good hearing.

13. c) Fish.
Gag groupers are only one of the 162 types of grouper fish. Because groupers are so yummy, they are one of the world's favorite fish to eat.

14. c) Giant squid.
You would have to go deep into the ocean to see a giant squid because they prefer to live at least 1,000 feet below the surface. They have such big eyes because it's very dark down there.

15. c) Cow.
Just like female elephants, female whales are called cows. Male whales and male elephants are both called bulls.

16. a) Electric eel.
The electric eel can grow up to eight feet long, but that's not the scariest part. Their ability to shock other animals is strong enough to knock down a full-grown man.

17. a) Stingray.
Just like its cousin, you don't want to mess with a stingray! They can grow over six feet long, and they use their spiky tails to inject venom.

18. a) Squid.
The ocean's squid are closely related to octopus. Both creatures have eight arms, but only the squid can squirt black ink at any predators that might try to eat it.

19. b) Stonefish.
Like the pufferfish, the stonefish is one of the world's most venomous creatures. They are often found clinging to rocks and reefs, but they tend to only use their poison to keep predators away.

20. b) Hermit crab.
All crabs have 10 legs, but hermit crabs are a little different. Instead of growing a full-body shell, they move into seashells that they carry on their backs.

21. c) Dolphin.
Dolphins are so smart that they have their own language. They use a series of sounds to echolocate both their food and their families.

22. a) Coral.
Corals serve a very important purpose in the ocean's food chain. Closely related to the jellyfish, there are more ocean creatures found in their reefs than there are birds on land.

23. c) Seahorses.
Baby seahorses are called fries, and they spend the first few weeks of their life floating alongside plankton. When they grow up, they rarely travel without a friend.

24. d) Humpback whale.
When you are 62 feet long and you weigh over 65,000 pounds, you don't need teeth! Humpback whales have something called baleen plates that allow them to suck in their food.

25. b) Pufferfish.
Whether you call it a blowfish, a pufferfish, or a bubblefish, it's one dangerous fish! One pufferfish has so much deadly venom that even fishermen won't touch their spikes.

26. a) They do belly flops.
If seals need to cross land, they flop on their bellies until they get where they need to go. Sea lions take a faster route by using all four flippers to walk.

27. b) Teeth.
Like sharks, lampreys don't have bones, but they do have a lot of teeth. They use all 12 rows of them to attach themselves to other fish and suck out all their blood.

28. c) Shrimp.
Like octopus and jellyfish, shrimp do not have spines. Their head and their thorax are joined together and protected by a shell.

29. a)Humuhumunukunukuapua'a
Believe it or not, the humuhumunukunukuapua'a doesn't have the longest name of all fish. The fish with the longest name is lauwiliwilinukunuku'oi'oi, and it lives in Hawaii too.

30. b) Hang out with other octopuses. Our eight-legged ocean friends are extremely smart, and they like to climb rocks, swim, and hide. But, they prefer to spend most of their life alone, and you'll rarely see them with another octopus.

Chapter 3

"I know the sky is not the limit because there are footprints on the Moon – and I made some of them!"
- Buzz Aldrin

Far out facts you'll want everyone to know!

1. Which one of the solar system's planets is the sun's closest neighbor?

a) Venus
b) Jupiter
c) Mercury
d) Uranus

2. If you were looking at the planet that has a big red spot, which planet would you be seeing?

a) Jupiter
b) Mars
c) Earth
d) Saturn

3. What do other planets have that Venus does not have?

a) Atmosphere
b) Dust
c) Moons
d) Gasses

4. What's the name of the planet that has rings made of ice, gas, and dust?

a) Mercury
b) Saturn
c) Jupiter
d) Venus

5. Shooting stars are also known by which one of these names?

a) Meteorite
b) Comet
c) Constellation
d) Stratosphere

6. How much money would you have to save to buy a NASA spacesuit?

a) $300
b) $12,000,000
c) $25,000
d) $23

7. What's the loudest thing you might hear while floating in outer space?

a) Silence
b) Sonic boom
c) Thunderstorm
d) Solar flare

8. Which one of these human things could you find on the moon?

a) Fingerprint
b) Footprint
c) Skin cell
d) Stray hair

9. Do you know what's happening inside Jupiter's red spot?

a) A storm
b) A volcano
c) An earthquake
d) A polar shift

10. How many times do you think the Earth rotates around the sun every day?

a) 24
b) 12
c) 1
d) 30

11. Can you figure out the tasty name of the galaxy we live in?

a) Ice Cream Zone
b) Milky Way
c) Lemonade Galaxy
d) Popsicle Highway

12. Do you know the name of the constellation that has three stars for a belt?

a) Big Dipper
b) Little Dipper
c) Orion
d) Gemini

13. If the sun isn't a planet, what is it?

a) Asteroid
b) Comet
c) Meteor
d) Star

14. What's the name of the rocks that are found floating in outer space?

a) Constellations
b) Planets
c) Asteroids
d)Black holes

15. Can you think of another name for the aurora borealis?

a) The light show
b) The Northern lights
c) The Eastern lights
d) The Western lights

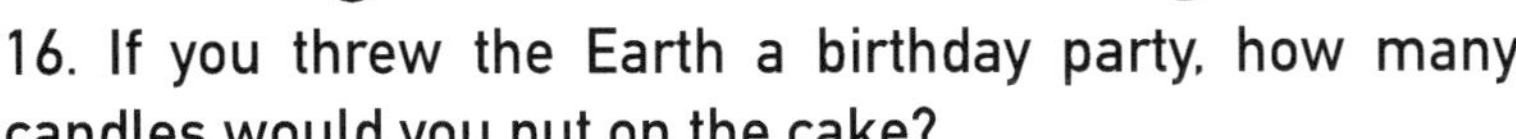

16. If you threw the Earth a birthday party, how many candles would you put on the cake?

a) 75
b) 1 million
c) 4.5 billion
d) 150

17. What's the term used when the Earth's shadow covers up the moon?

a) Lunar eclipse
b) Wolf moon
c) Northern Lights
d) Solar eclipse

18. Which of these nicknames is given to Mars?

a) The Fast Planet
b) The Rosy Planet
c) The Red Planet
d) The Round Planet

19. What name is given to the part of a comet you see trailing behind it?

a) Tail
b) Bumper
c) Meteor
d) Shooting star

20. Which one of these countries was the first to send someone into orbit?

a) Brazil
b) United States
c) Russia
d) China

21. Do you have any idea which one of these planets has at least 67 moons?

a) Jupiter
b) Earth
c) Uranus
d) Mars

22. What's the name of the force that keeps us from floating away into space?

a) Centrifugal
b) Gravity
c) Weight
d) Muscle

23. Do you know which type of black hole is the biggest?

a) Supermassive black hole
b) Enormous black hole
c) Stellar black hole
d) Primordial black hole

24. Which one of these planets is the coldest because it's furthest away from the sun?

a) Neptune
b) Mars
c) Pluto
d) Saturn

25. Can you guess the longest amount of time any astronaut has spent in space?

a) 2 decades
b) 16 years
c) 12 hours
d) 665 days

26. Can you figure out which one of these is NOT the name of a NASA space shuttle?

a) Discovery
b) Enterprise
c) Columbia
d) Air Force One

27. How long do you think it takes for the sun's warm rays to reach the Earth?

a) 3 years
b) 30 years
c) 300 years
d) 8 minutes

28. Which one of these planets prefers to rotate on its side?

a) Earth
b) Venus
c) Uranus
d) Neptune

29. What's the name of the gas that Earth has but other planets lack?

a) Oxygen
b) Nitrogen
c) Helium
d) Carbon dioxide

30. How many times does a lunar eclipse take place?

a) Once a year
b) Never, it is a myth
c) Every month
d) At least twice a year

ANSWER

1. c) Mercury.
Mercury might sit closest to the sun, but it's not the hottest planet. With temperatures that go over 700°F, Venus gets slightly hotter.

2. a) Jupiter.
Jupiter is the biggest planet in our solar system. It's so big that it can hold 1,300 Earths inside it!

3. c) Moons.
There are two things that make Venus a special planet. Not only is it the hottest planet, it's also the only planet that doesn't have moons.

4. b) Saturn.
Saturn is the sixth planet from the sun, and it's easy to recognize by its rings. The rings were discovered in the 1600s, but no one has ever figured out how they got there.

5. a) Meteorite.
When you see a shooting star streak across the sky, you are technically seeing a meteorite — a meteor that has entered the earth's atmosphere.

6. b) $12,000,000.
You would have to save for a long time to have enough money for an astronaut's suit, and you would need a lot of muscles to wear it. Each suit weighs 47 pounds and costs $12 million dollars!

7. a) Silence.
Since space doesn't have an atmosphere, there's no way for sound waves to travel. The loudest think you would hear there is silence.

8. b) Footprint.
The footprints of the astronauts from Apollo 11 have been there since they landed in 1969. There's no wind on the moon, so they will remain there for at least 100 million years.

9. a) A storm.
Jupiter's giant red spot is shrinking. The raging storms taking place there seem to be breaking it up.

10. c) 1.
The Earth spins at 1,000 miles per hour, but it only goes around the sun once per day. Mercury rotates around the sun four times.

11. b) Milky Way.
Our entire solar system sits inside the Milky Way. Scientists think there are between 200 and 400 million stars in the Milky Way, but it's impossible to count them all.

12. c) Orion.
Legend has it that Orion was one of Zeus' mythological hunters before he was turned into a constellation. His belt is made from three stars named Alnilam, Mintaka, and Alnitak.

13. d) Star.
The sun is such a big star that one million Earths could sit inside it. Some scientists believe that the sun will eventually absorb the Earth.

14. c) Asteroids.
There are an estimated 600,000 asteroids orbiting the sun. The first one ever discovered was named Ceres.

15. b) The Northern lights.
The aurora borealis, or the Northern Lights, is a colorful display that happens when electrons in the Earth's magnetic field are agitated. Sunspots can cause them to be more active.

16. c) 4.5 billion.
Rocks found in Canada have led scientists to believe that Earth is around 4.5 billion years old. You would need a huge cake for all those candles!

17. a) Lunar eclipse.
Unlike a solar eclipse, you can watch a lunar eclipse without special glasses. Lunar eclipses can last for hours.

18. c) The Red Planet.
Mars is also called the Red Planet because its soil is full of iron that oxidizes. This process gives the planet a red hue.

19. a) Tail.
Comets orbit the sun just like the planets. They have four parts and two of them are known as tails.

20. c) Russia.
In 1961, a Russian spacecraft named Vostok carried one man into orbit. The United States sent astronaut Alan Shepard into orbit later the same year.

21. a) Jupiter.
Throughout our solar system, there are over 180 moons. While the Earth only has one, Jupiter has at least 67.

22. b) Gravity.
You can thank gravity for keeping you from floating away. Gravity's force is a natural occurrence that keeps all the planets and moons in orbit.

23. a) Supermassive black hole.
Supermassive black holes are so huge that they are over a million times bigger than the sun. You can't see them, though.

24. a) Neptune.
Neptune is the fourth biggest planet and gets less of the sun's warmth than other planets. All of its surface is made from ice.

25. d) 665 days.
In 2017, an American astronaut named Patty Whiston set a new record. She spent 665 days on the space station!

26. d) Air Force One.
There have been six total space shuttles, and they are named Discovery, Challenger, Enterprise, Columbia, Atlantis, and Endeavor. Air Force One is the plane the American president flies on.

27. d) 8 minutes.
If you think about all the miles the sun's rays have to travel, it's amazing that they get here in only eight minutes. Thankfully, all that traveling and our atmosphere cools them down before they arrive.

28. c) Uranus.
In 1781, Uranus was the first planet discovered through a telescope. The gasses in the atmospheric layers of Uranus make it appear blue.

29. a) Oxygen.
Life as we know it is supported by the Earth's oxygen supply. If they have any at all, other planets lack enough of it to support human life.

30. d) At least twice a year.
A lunar eclipse takes place when the Earth blocks the sun light from hitting the moon. The Earth, Moon and Sun have to be in a straight line for this to take place.

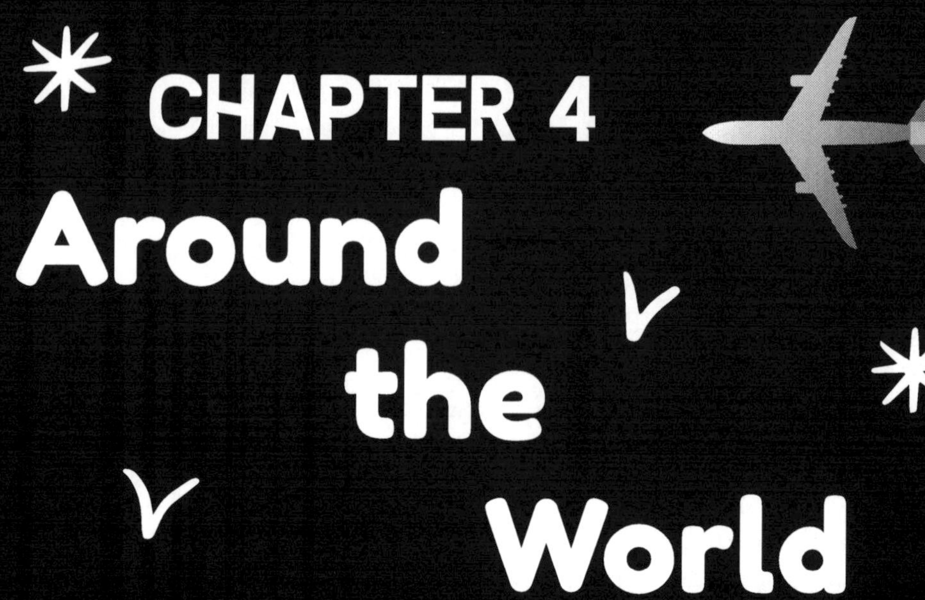

CHAPTER 4 Around the World

"YOU'RE OFF TO GREAT PLACES. TODAY IS YOUR DAY. YOUR MOUNTAIN IS WAITING SO GET ON YOUR WAY." ~ DR. SEUSS

Learn about here, there, and everywhere!

1. Brisbane, Sydney, and Adelaide are major cities in which country?

a) Australia
b) Luxembourg
c) Peru
d) Canada

2. Which language is the world's most commonly spoken?

a) Spanish
b) Chinese
c) English
d) French

3. What's the name of the country that isn't located in Europe?

a) Italy
b) Denmark
c) Japan
d) England

4. Which of these continents is home to the country of Kenya?

a) North America
b) Asia
c) Antarctica
d) Africa

5. Which one of these gulfs sits off Florida's western coast?

a) Gulf of Mexico
b) The Persian Gulf
c) Gulf of Alaska
d) Gulf of Guinea

6. Which one of these natural disasters occurs when there's an earthquake under the ocean?

a) Typhoon
b) Hurricane
c) Tornado
d) Tsunami

7. What's the name of the science that studies the earth's features?

a) Biology
b) Geography
c) Phlebotomy
d) Botany

8. What's the name of the big gorge carved in the American Southwest?

a) Grand Gorge
b) Gorge Canyon
c) Grand Canyon
d) Canyon Gorge

9. Which one of these mountain ranges is the oldest in the United States?

a) Appalachian Mountains
b) Rocky Mountains
c) Sierra Nevada Mountains
d) White Mountains

10. Do you know which country does not belong in Scandinavia?

a) Chile
b) Norway
c) Denmark
d) Sweden

11. Which continent is home to the world's largest and oldest rainforest?

a) Australia
b) North America
c) Europe
d) South America

12. Can you guess which U.S. state gets less rainfall that all the others?

a) Hawaii
b) Florida
c) Nevada
d) Alaska

13. Brooklyn, The Bronx, and Harlem are boroughs in which major city?

a) New York
b) Chicago
c) Los Angeles
d) Miami

14. Which one of these oceans is the smallest one in the world?

a) Pacific
b) Arctic
c) Atlantic
d) Indian

15. Which of these islands is home to the Statue of Liberty?
a) Puerto Rico
b) Hawaii
c) Liberty Island
d) Manhattan

16. What's the name of the mountain that's sometimes called the Jewel of the Swiss Alps?
a) Mount Everest
b) Matterhorn
c) Mount Kilauea
d) Mount Olympus

17. Do you know which of the United Kingdom's countries created the legend of leprechauns?
a) Wales
b) Ireland
c) Scotland
d) England

18. Which one of these geography words means a "small piece of land completely surrounded by water?"
a) Isthmus
b) Island
c) Peninsula
d) Plateau

19. Which U.S. state can some Russians see with a pair of binoculars?

a) Alaska
b) California
c) Washington
d) Oregon

20. The capital city of Mexico is sinking; what's the name of it?

a) Tijuana
b) Merida
c) Mexico City
d) Cancun

21. What famous national park sits on top of a supervolcano?

a) Denali
b) Yellowstone
c) Joshua Tree
d) Everglades

22. Do you have any idea which of these cities is the world's oldest?

a) Damascus
b) Los Angeles
c) London
d) Rio De Janeiro

23. Can you guess which one of these countries eats the most cheese?

a) Uruguay
b) Bolivia
c) France
d) Egypt

24. Istanbul, Turkey sits on two continents; which two?

a) Africa and Asia
b) North and Central America
c) Europe and Asia
d) Australia and Antarctica

25. What's the name of the country that Alaska borders?

a) Russia
b) Japan
c) Greenland
d) Canada

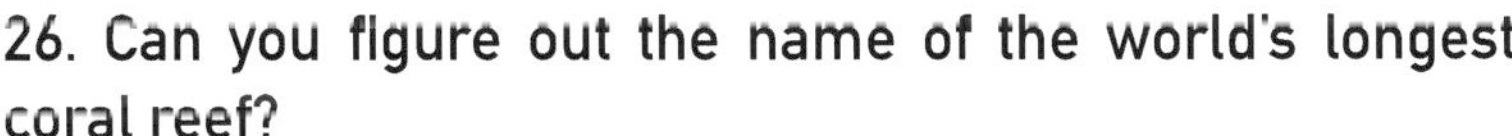

26. Can you figure out the name of the world's longest coral reef?

a) Great Big Reef
b) Great Ocean Reef
c) Big Great Reef
d) Great Barrier Reef

27. What's the name of the country that gets the most tornadoes?

a) Costa Rica
b) Thailand
c) South Africa
d) United States

28. What's the name of the popular waterfalls between the U.S. and Canada?

a) Victoria Falls
b) Niagara Falls
c) Angel Falls
d) Cathedral Falls

29. What U.S. state shares its name with the biggest river in the country?

a) Mississippi
b) Montana
c) North Carolina
d) Connecticut

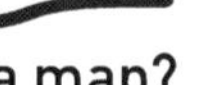

30. Where would you find the Bermuda Triangle on a map?

a) Atlantic Ocean
b) Pacific Ocean
c) Caspian Sea
d) Mediterranean Sea

ANSWER

1. a) Australia.
With over 5 million people, Sydney is Australia's biggest city. Australia sits in the southern hemisphere, and it's also one of the seven continents.

2. b) Chinese.
Across the world there are around 6,500 languages spoken, and Chinese is the most popular. Over 900 million people speak a version of it called Mandarin Chinese!

3. c) Japan.
There are 44 countries in Europe, but Japan isn't one of them. Japan is an island nation, and it's considered part of Asia.

4. d) Africa.
To find Kenya on a map, you would need to look for the African continent. Africa is home to the world's longest river and the hottest desert.

5. a) Gulf of Mexico.
There are 62 gulfs around the world, and Florida rests on the Gulf of Mexico. The saltwater there is four times more salty than the nearby Atlantic Ocean.

6. d) Tsunami.
When an earthquake strikes on the ocean's floor, a huge wall of water called a tsunami ripples throughout the region. In 1958, a tsunami that stood 1,720 feet tall reached Alaska.

7. b) Geography.
If you grow up to study all the world's atmosphere, landscape, and resources, you'll take a lot of geography classes. You could specialize in either physical, human, or environmental geography.

8. c) Grand Canyon.
Running through Arizona, the Grand Canyon measures 270 miles long. It took the Colorado River millions of years to carve it.

9. a) Appalachian Mountains.
The Appalachian Mountains run all the way from Maine to Georgia. Since they were created over 480 million years ago, they are considered the oldest mountains in the world.

10. a) Chile.
The Scandinavian countries of Norway, Denmark, and Sweden are the northernmost countries in Europe. Chile sits halfway around the world in South America.

11. d) South America.
Some of the plants in animals in the Amazon rainforest date back over 70 million years! You would have to travel to South American to see them for yourself.

12. c) Nevada.
Even though Nevada's name means "snow-capped," it gets less rain than any other state. Unlike Hawaii that gets 404 inches of rain every year, Nevada gets less than 10!

13. a) New York.
With a population over 8.3 million people, New York is one of the world's most populated cities. Including Staten Island and Queens, there are five boroughs within the city.

14. b) Arctic.
Out of all five oceans, the Arctic Ocean is the smallest. It borders the United States, Canada, and Russia, amongst other places.

15. c) Liberty Island.
When the Statue of Liberty was given as a gift by France, it was built on Bedloe's Island. In 1956, it was renamed Liberty Island, and you'll have to take a ferry to get there.

16. b) Matterhorn.
Rising out of The Alps in Switzerland, the Matterhorn almost looks like a pyramid. When translated into English, Matterhorn means meadow peak.

17. b) Ireland.
Ireland is the home of a lot of legends and leprechauns. It's the 20th biggest island in the world, and over 6 million people live there.

18. b) Island.
Unlike peninsulas that only have water on three sides, islands are completely surrounded. Greenland is the world's largest of them all.

19. a) Alaska.
Russia and Alaska are only 55 miles apart, but they are separated by a powerful body of water called the Bering Strait.

20. c) Mexico City.
Around 1325 AD, The Aztecs filled in a lake to build Mexico City. Over the past 70 years, it has sunken over 30 feet!

21. b) Yellowstone.
Thankfully, the supervolcano beneath Yellowstone hasn't exploded in almost 650,000 years. The geysers and hot springs are signs that it's still active, though.

22. a) Damascus.
Built over 11,000 years ago, Damascus, Syria is the world's oldest. Jerusalem and Athens come in second and third place.

23. c) France.
France is the cheese-eating capital of the world. It's estimated that the average French person will eat over 56 pounds of it a year!

24. c) Europe and Asia.
Istanbul is a unique city that has been the home to several empires for over 2,000 years. Part of it sits in Europe and part of it sits in Asia.

25. d) Canada.
Including the eastern side of Alaska, the United States and Canada share the world's longest border. It stretches for 3,987 total miles!

26 d) Great Barrier Reef.
Right off the coast of Australia and in the middle of Coral Sea, The Great Barrier Reef is approximately 1,429 miles long, and over 1,500 different fish like to hang out there.

27. d) United States.
Tornadoes happen so frequently in the United States that that part of the country is nicknamed Tornado Alley. Each season, there are around 180 tornadoes spotted.

28. b) Niagara Falls.
Every year, nearly 30 million people head to Niagara Falls to watch over 3,000 gallons of water per second tumble over the natural formation.

29. a) Mississippi.
The Mississippi River starts in Minnesota and travels through 10 states. It meets the Gulf of Mexico in the state of Mississippi.

30. a) Atlantic Ocean.
Since the 1950s, the Bermuda Triangle has been one of the Atlantic Ocean's biggest mysteries. Many ships and aircrafts have disappeared there.

The Human Body
Chapter 5

"The human body is the most complex system ever created. The more we learn about it, the more appreciation we have about what a rich system it is."
~ Bill Gates

Can you look at your body and get all these right?

1. How many teeth do you think a fully grown adult has?

a) 10 b) 311

c) 32 d) 5

2. Which one of these things are your ears and your nose made out of?

a) Bone b) Muscle

c) Cartilage d) Marrow

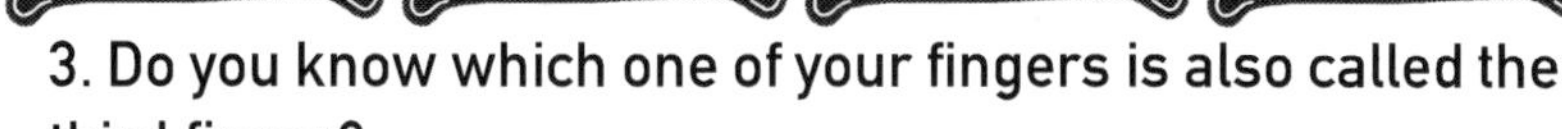

3. Do you know which one of your fingers is also called the third finger?

a) Thumb b) Middle

c) Index d) Pinky

4. Your tongue has around 10,000 of which of these things?

a) Hairs b) Taste buds

c) Layers d) Muscles

5. What's another name for the bony cranium that protects your brain?

a) Helmet
b) Scalp
c) Skull
d) Noggin

6. Can you guess which one of your organs is the biggest?

a) Skin
b) Heart
c) Brain
d) Pancreas

7. Which spongy organ has parts named cerebellum and cerebral cortex?

a) Brain
b) Liver
c) Intestines
d) Lungs

8. Which liquid does your body produce over six cups of every day?

a) Spit
b) Sweat
c) Urine
d) Stomach acid

9. What part of your body is either A, B, O, or AB type?

a) Lungs
b) Blood
c) Liver
d) Appendix

10. Which one of your body parts is over 20 feet long when stretched out?

a) Gallbladder
b) Heart
c) Small intestines
d) Spine

11. You use 43 of your face muscles when you do what?

a) Laugh
b) Frown
c) Smile
d) Sip

12. Which of these things was attached to an umbilical cord before you were born?

a) Belly button
b) Nose
c) Lips
d) Knee

13. How long does it take for your body to completely digest your food?

a) 10 minutes
b) 4 weeks
c) 1 month
d) 2 to 5 days

14. What's it called when someone can't see certain colors?

a) Color blind
b) Grayness
c) Black and white vision
d) Blue sight

15. Where do you think you would find your body's strongest muscle?

a) Thigh
b) Jaw
c) Abdomen
d) Shoulder

16. What's your body's normal temperature in degrees Fahrenheit?

a) 101.8
b) 32
c) 98.6
d) 212

17. Which of these body parts is impossible to lick?

a) Heel
b) Knee
c) Elbow
d) Wrist

18. Can you guess which of these things is the hardest part of your body?

a) Tooth enamel
b) Bones
c) Bone marrow
d) Cartilage

19. Where would you find three little bones called the hammer, anvil, and stirrup?

a) Foot
b) Ear
c) Hand
d) Spine

20. You have 26 of which things in your feet?
a) Blood cells
b) Cuticles
c) Bones
d) Veins

21. Which part of your skeleton protects your lungs?
a) Rib cage
b) Skull
c) Girdles
d) Appendages

22. Which one of these is not part of your eye?
a) Lens
b) Iris
c) Palate
d) Pupil

23. Where would you find bones called vertebrae?
a) Hand
b) Ear
c) Skull
d) Spine

24. Which one of your organs can be affected by asthma?
a) Lungs
b) Stomach
c) Liver
d) Large intestine

25. What part of your body has chambers, vessels, and valves?
a) Brain
b) Heart
c) Colon
d) Mouth

26. What happens to your spine when you go into outer space?
a) It gets shorter.
b) It curls up.
c) It gets longer.
d) It stays the same

27. What part of your body is home to muscles called triceps and biceps?

a) Hips
b) Legs
c) Neck
d) Arms

28. Which one of your prints is strangely close to a koala's print?

a) Fingerprint
b) Tongue print
c) Footprint
d) Nose print

29. Where might you find a hard substance known as keratin?

a) Bladder
b) Stomach
c) Toenails
d) Tongue

30. Aside from your fingers, what part of your body makes a print that's unique to you?

a) Knee
b) Tongue
c) Foot
d) Elbow

ANSWER

1. c) 32.
Before they fall out and become adult teeth, you have 20 baby teeth. When you're an adult, you will have 32.

2. c) Cartilage.
Both your nose and your ears are made of a flexible and tough thing called cartilage. If you were a shark, all of your bones would be made from it too.

3. b) Middle.
In the anatomy books, the middle finger is labeled as the third finger of your hand. It's always the longest human finger.

4. b) Taste buds.
Your tongue is one big muscle, and it's covered by 10,000 taste buds. As you get older, the number of them gets smaller.

5. c) Skull.
Your brain is protected by 22 bones that fuse together to make your skull. It doesn't stop growing until you are between six and 12 years old.

6. a) Skin.
Your skin is made up of three different layers, and it's the biggest organ. The epidermis, or outer layer, is always thicker on your hands and feet.

7. a) Brain.
When your brain has finished growing, it weighs about three pounds. It's such a busy organ that it uses 20% of your body's total energy.

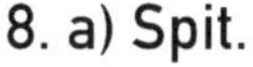

8. a) Spit.
Every day, your salivary glands make over six cups of spit! Also called saliva, it's the first step in breaking down your food.

9. b) Blood.
Even though there are over 30 total blood types, they are usually classified by the letters A, B, and O. Your blood makes up 7% of your body's total weight.

10. c) Small intestines.
Although the small intestines of both men and women are over 20 feet long, women's are a little longer. On average, their small intestines stretch over 23 feet!

11. b) Frown.
Although the exact number varies, it takes at least 43 muscles to frown. It only takes 26 to smile — so smile!

12. a) Belly button.
Your navel, or belly button, used to connect you to your mom with the umbilical cord. It provided all the blood and nutrients you needed to grow.

13. d) 2 to 5 days.
From the time you swallow your food, it takes between two and five days for it to reach the other end. Your stomach, small intestines, and large intestines are responsible for the task.

14. a) Color blind.
Around 1 in 12 people are color blind and lack the ability to see certain colors. They have a hard time telling the difference between blues, greens, and oranges.

15. b) Jaw.
Located on the bottom of your jaw, the masseter is your body's strongest muscle. It helps your teeth bite down with up to 200 pounds of pressure!

16. c) 98.6.
If you have a normal temperature, the thermometer will read 98.6°F. When it goes higher, it might mean you have an illness or infection.

17. c) Elbow.
You can try, but it's impossible to lick your own elbow. If you could, you would be able to use your tongue's taste zones to see if it was sweet, salty, sour, or bitter.

18. a) Tooth enamel.
Fueled by minerals like calcium,your tooth enamel is the hardest. It's important to brush because acids and bacteria can cause it to wear away over time.

19. b) Ear.
Your ear is home to the smallest bones in your body. Sitting behind your eardrum, they vibrate from all the sounds you hear.

20. c) Bones.
Each of your feet is made up of 26 different bones. The rounded heel bone is the strongest of them all.

21. a) Rib cage.
Your rib cage does a great job at protecting most of your upper organs like the lungs. You have 24 rib bones that form the cage.

22. c) Palate.
The palate is the upper part of your mouth, but all the rest are parts of your eye. The lens is the only part that never stops growing.

23. d) Spine.
Each one of your spine's vertebrae has a hole for the spinal cord to fit. Humans have 33, but only 24 of them move.

24. a) Lungs.
When someone has an asthma attack, they have a hard time breathing. It affects the lung's airways by making them more narrow.

25. b) Heart.
Your heart has four chambers that house the vessels and valves that keep your blood moving. Over a year's time, it beats around 35 million times!

26. c) It gets longer.
Because there's no gravity in space, your spine gets longer and you get taller. Being weightless allows the cartilage between your spine's bones to stretch.

27. d) Arms.
Triceps and biceps make up the big muscles of your upper arms. There are around 20 muscles that make your forearms and hands work.

28. a) Fingerprint.
Your fingerprint is unique to only you, but koala bears have very similar prints. In fact, their fingerprints have been confused for human fingerprints at some crime scenes.

29. c) Toenails.
Your hair isn't as hard as your nails, but both of them are made from keratin. The hooves of horses and cows are too.

30. b) Tongue.
Just like your fingerprints, your tongue print has a series of markers that belong only to you. Tongue prints are becoming a popular way to identify people. geography.

Holidays and Traditions

"The holiday season is a perfect time to reflect on our blessings and seek out ways to make life better for those around us."
~ Anonymous

Can you beat your best friend by knowing more about holidays?

1. What's the name of the holiday some countries celebrate on December 26?

a) Wrapping Day
b) Ribbon Day
c) Boxing Day
d) Package Day

2. How many reindeer does Santa have pulling his sleigh on Christmas Eve?

a) 23
b) 9
c) 1
d) 15

3. Which holiday bird does the U.S. President pardon every year?

a) Partridge
b) Goose
c) Turkey
d) Chicken

4. Do you know what a pumpkin becomes when it's carved for Halloween?

a) Jack o'lantern
b) Pumpkinhead
c) Scarecrow
d) Shrunken head

5. What's the name of the song that plays when the ball drops on New Year's Eve?

a) "Auld Lang Syne"
b) "Happy Birthday"
c) "The Star Spangled Banner"
d) "Jingle Bells"

______ ____ _____ ______ ____ _____

6. Which June holiday celebrates one of your parents?

a) Father's Day
b) Mom Day
c) Dad Day
d) Man Day

______ ____ _____ ______ ____ _____

7. Do you know which colorful holiday is celebrated between December 26 and New Year's Day?

a) Kwanzaa
b) Hanukkah
c) Lunar New Year
d) Ramadan

______ ____ _____ ______ ____ _____

8. What's the name of the Hindu festival of lights that's celebrated every November?

a) Thanksgiving
b) Diwali
c) Lights Day
d) Chalk Day

______ ____ _____ ______ ____ _____

9. Which one of these holidays takes place closest to the winter solstice?

a) Christmas
b) Halloween
c) New Years Day
d) Valentine's Day

______ ____ _____ ______ ____ _____

10. Which Jewish celebration involves lighting nine candles?

a) Diwali
b) Ramadan
c) Hanukkah
d) Kwanzaa

______ ____ _____ ______ ____ _____

11. Do you know which cold month Rubber Ducky Day takes place in?

a) June
b) September
c) January
d) March

12. What is traditionally given inside red envelopes during Chinese New Year?

a) Playing cards
b) Money
c) Ribbons
d) Confetti

13. Hot dogs and fireworks are a huge part of which US patriotic holiday?

a) 4th of July
b) Veterans Day
c) President's Day
d) Fireworks Day

14. Which American city is famous for its giant Mardi Gras floats?

a) Tulsa
b) New Orleans
c) Indianapolis
d) Cleveland

15. What kind of fruit is used to make a popular Thanksgiving sauce?

a) Blackberry
b) Lime
c) Cranberry
d) Black currant

16. Which of these magical Halloween costumes is the most popular?

a) Witch
b) Cat
c) Zombie
d) Pirate

17. Can you figure out what they call Santa in The Netherlands?

a) Father Christmas
b) Sinterklaas
c) Old Man Christmas
d) Beardy Claus

18. What's the name of the holiday that always falls on the first Monday in September in America?

a) Labor Day
b) Flag Day
c) Memorial Day
d) Martin Luther King Day

19. What's the name of the Brazilian festival that happens around Easter?

a) Carnival
b) Hanukkah
c) Mother's Day
d) Cinco de Mayo

20. Any idea what oranges in stockings are said to represent?

a) Happiness
b) Love
c) Gold coins
d) Health

21. Can you figure out which one of these foods is a Hanukkah favorite?

a) Donuts
b) Asparagus
c) Raisins
d) Artichokes

22. What's the name of the Civil Rights leader we celebrate every January 18th?

a) John Lewis
b) Rosa Parks
c) Martin Luther King. Jr.
d) Barack Obama

23. Do you know the name of the Mexican holiday that's celebrated on May 5th?

a) May Day
b) Mother's Day
c) Cinco de Mayo
d) Memorial Day

24. What holiday honors a family member and happens in May?

a) Sister's Day
b) Brother's Day
c) Father's Day
d) Mother's Day

25. Do you know the name of the flower that's associated with Memorial Day?

a) Orchid
b) Marigold
c) Poppy
d) Rose

26. Baskets, hidden eggs, and nice clothes are a part of which springtime celebration?

a) Valentine's Day
b) Memorial Day
c) Easter
d) President's Day

27. Do you know the name of the cherub who shoots arrows on Valentine's Day?

a) Cupid
b) Blixen
c) Buddy
d) Leonard

28. What's the name of the November holiday that honors those who have served in the military?

a) Veterans Day
b) Thanksgiving
c) Labor Day
d) Army Day

29. What's another word for the Christmas item known as a tannenbaum?

a) Tree
b) Ornament
c) Carol
d) Gift

30. Feliz Navidad means Happy Christmas in which language?

a) French
b) Spanish
c) Italian
d) Portugeuse

ANSWER

1.c) Boxing Day.
On the day after Christmas, countries like England and Canada celebrate Boxing Day. It's a tradition that dates all the way back to when servants were given gifts in boxes.

2. b) 9.
There are a total of nine reindeer flying in front of Santa's sleigh. Rudolph always leads, but he's backed up by Donner, Dasher, Vixen, Dancer, Prancer, Comet, Cupid and Blitzen.

3. c) Turkey.
Since 1989, it's been a White House tradition to pardon a turkey before Thanksgiving. The lucky turkey returns to the farm rather than becoming a meal.

4. a) Jack o'lantern.
During the Halloween season, over 1.5 billion pounds of pumpkins are sold! While many are carved to become jack o'lanterns, some are used for decoration or pies.

5. a) "Auld Lang Syne".
At the stroke of midnight, many people sing "Auld Lang Syne." It marks the changing of years on our Gregorian calendar.

6. a) Father's Day.
Nearly 72 million greeting cards are given to dads around the world on Father's Day. The tradition started in 1912.

7. a) Kwanzaa.
With a name that means "first fruits of the season," Kwanzaa lasts for seven days. Each of the days corresponds to one of the holiday's seven principals.

8. b) Diwali.
Considered a day of new beginnings, Diwali is celebrated by millions of people all over the world. The festival involves food, dancing, and colorful chalk throwing.

9. a) Christmas.
The summer solstice marks the longest day of the year, and the winter solstice marks the shortest. Since it happens on December 21st, Christmas is the closest holiday.

10. c) Hanukkah.
Hanukkah is also called the Festival of Lights. Each day of the celebration is marked with a candle, and there are nine candles on the menorah by the time it's done.

11. c) January.
Rubber Ducky Day has been celebrated every January 13th since 1970. Made out of vulcanized rubber, they are one of the world's favorite toys.

12.b) Money.
The Chinese New Year is a celebration that takes place during winter. Friends and loved ones are given red envelopes with money inside, and they symbolize good fortune.

13. a) 4th of July.
Since 1777, fireworks have been used to celebrate America's birthday. July 4, 1776 is the date the Declaration of Independence was signed at Independence Hall in Philadelphia.

14. b) New Orleans.
A lot of cities hold Mardi Gras celebrations, but New Orleans is famous for their huge parties. Close to 1.5 million people attend every year.

15. c) Cranberry.
During the Thanksgiving season, over 80 million pounds of cranberries are sold. Most of them go into making cranberry sauce.

16. a) Witch.
There's a reason you see a lot of pointy hats and brooms on Halloween. Nearly 5 million people choose to be a witch!

17. b) Sinterklaas.
In the Netherlands, Sinterklaas visits children and delivers presents. Instead of reindeer, Sinterklaas has a big, white horse.

18. a) Labor Day.
Labor Day is an American holiday that honors the workforce. First celebrated in 1882, it's also the unofficial beginning of NFL season.
.

19. a) Carnival.
On the Friday before Ash Wednesday, millions of Brazilians take to the streets to celebrate Carnival. The festivities are full of colorful outfits, food, and music.

20. c) Gold coins.
Legend says that the sacks Saint Nicholas threw down the chimney spilled gold coins into the stockings on the mantle. Today, oranges represent those coins.

21. a) Donuts.
Donuts are a Hanukkah tradition. In fact, they each over 1.5 million of them in Israel over the course of the festival.

22. c) Martin Luther King, Jr..
Martin Luther King, Jr.'s birthday is January 15, but we celebrate his humanitarian work every January 18th. During the 1960s, his voice led the way for equality.

23. c) Cinco de Mayo.
Typically, Cinco de Mayo is celebrated more in the United States. Mexico prefers to celebrate its independence day in September.

24. d) Mother's Day.
President Woodrow Wilson declared Mother's Day an official holiday in 1912. Mothers are showered with over $25 billion worth of gifts every year.

25. c) Poppy.
After WWI, red poppies were the first flowers to grow in abandoned battlefields. Since then, the flower has been worn to symbolize remembrance.

26. c) Easter.
Every year, the Easter bunny spends about $2 billion on candy. Even though the holiday is a Christian celebration that goes back a long time, the bunny's only 400 or 500 years old.

27. a) Cupid.
Valentine's Day is a 600-year-old tradition! Although it hasn't always been associated with love, Cupid has been around since the Romans created the holiday.

28. a) Veterans Day.
When Veterans Day was signed into law in 1919, it was called Armistice Day. It was created to honor the sacrifice of soldiers, sailors, and airmen.

29. a) Tree.
Tannenbaum is the German word for Christmas tree. There are around 30 million Christmas trees sold every year.

30. b) Spanish.
Spanish speakers all over the world say "Feliz Navidad!" If you wanted to wish someone a good new year, you would say, "Feliz Nuevo Ano."

Chapter 7

Food And Drinks

"Nothing brings people together like GOOD FOOD" ~Annoymous

Food facts are fun facts!

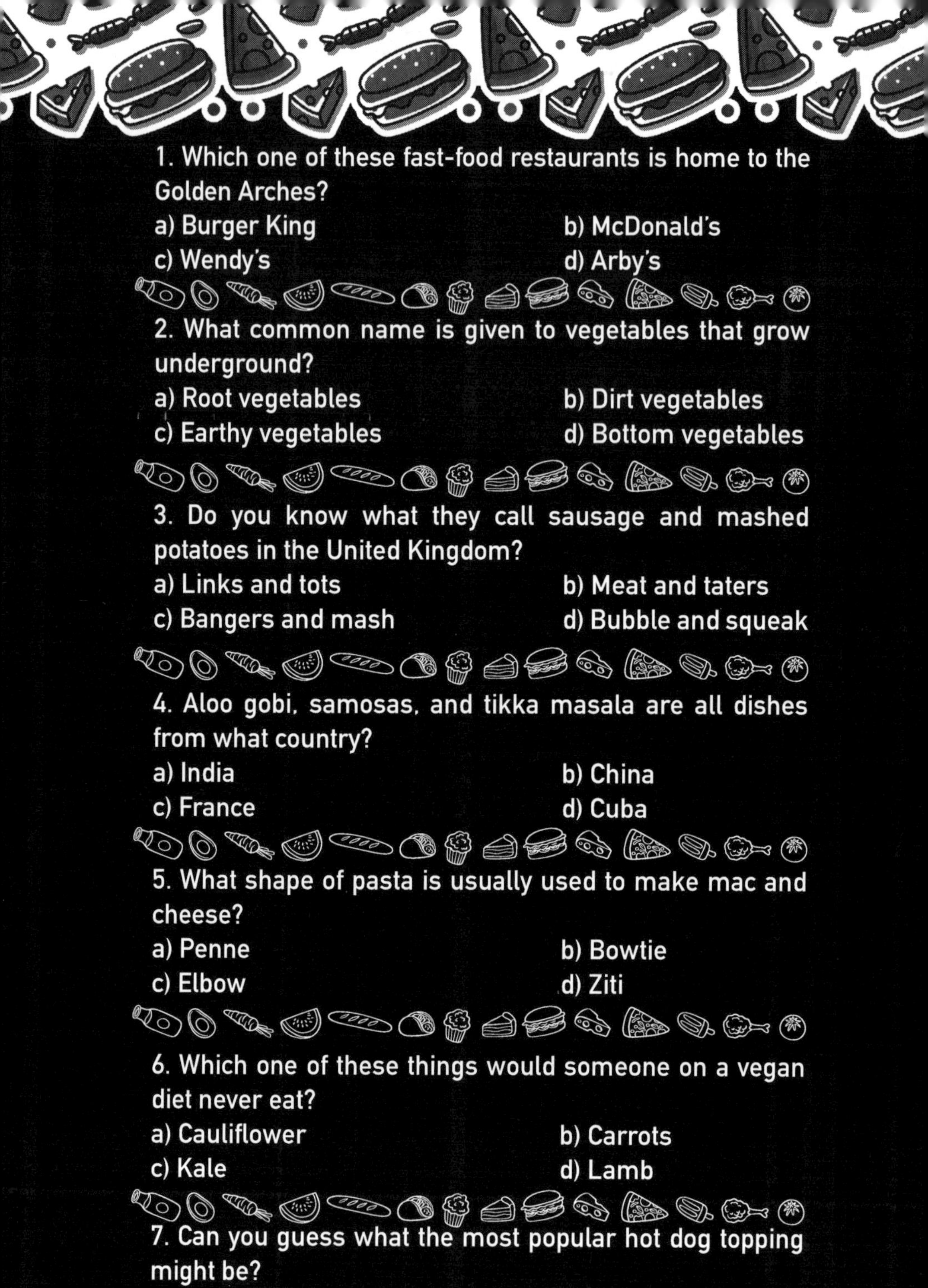

1. Which one of these fast-food restaurants is home to the Golden Arches?

a) Burger King
b) McDonald's
c) Wendy's
d) Arby's

2. What common name is given to vegetables that grow underground?

a) Root vegetables
b) Dirt vegetables
c) Earthy vegetables
d) Bottom vegetables

3. Do you know what they call sausage and mashed potatoes in the United Kingdom?

a) Links and tots
b) Meat and taters
c) Bangers and mash
d) Bubble and squeak

4. Aloo gobi, samosas, and tikka masala are all dishes from what country?

a) India
b) China
c) France
d) Cuba

5. What shape of pasta is usually used to make mac and cheese?

a) Penne
b) Bowtie
c) Elbow
d) Ziti

6. Which one of these things would someone on a vegan diet never eat?

a) Cauliflower
b) Carrots
c) Kale
d) Lamb

7. Can you guess what the most popular hot dog topping might be?

a) Mustard
b) Onions
c) Relish
d) Ketchup

8. What's the name of the food most often associated with Japan?

a) Shepherd's pie
b) Sushi
c) Hot dogs
d) Tikka Masala

9. Which food do you think is considered a stone fruit?

a) Peach
b) Cabbage
c) Grape
d) Broccoli

10. Do you know the name of the German side dish that's made with cabbage and salt?

a) Schnitzel
b) Pretzel
c) Sauerkraut
d) Gherkin

11. What's the name of the donut-shaped bread that New Yorker's love?

a) Bagel
b) Baguette
c) Potato bun
d) Eclair

12. What's the name of the food that's said to keep vampires away?

a) Pumpkin
b) Sauerkraut
c) Garlic
d) Cantaloupe

13. If you wanted to have a small Frosty for dessert, which restaurant would you go to?

a) Subway
b) Wendy's
c) Taco Bell
d) IHOP

14. What's the name of the condiment that's made from tomatoes, sugar, and vinegar?

a) Ketchup
b) Mustard
c) Mayonnaise
d) Relish

15. Do you know which one of these herbs is commonly used to make pickles?

a) Basil
b) Oregano
c) Dill
d) Parsley

16. What's the name of the drink that's made by blending ice cream and milk together?

a) Cappuccino b) Seltzer
c) Slushie d) Milkshake

17. What makes the blue or green parts in blue cheese?

a) Seeds b) Mold
c) Sauce d) Food coloring

18. When chocolate starts life on the cacao tree, what part of the tree is it?

a) Leaf b) Bark
c) Root d) Seed

19. Americans eat 350 slices of what favorite food every second?

a) Cheese b) Pizza
c) Pie d) Apple

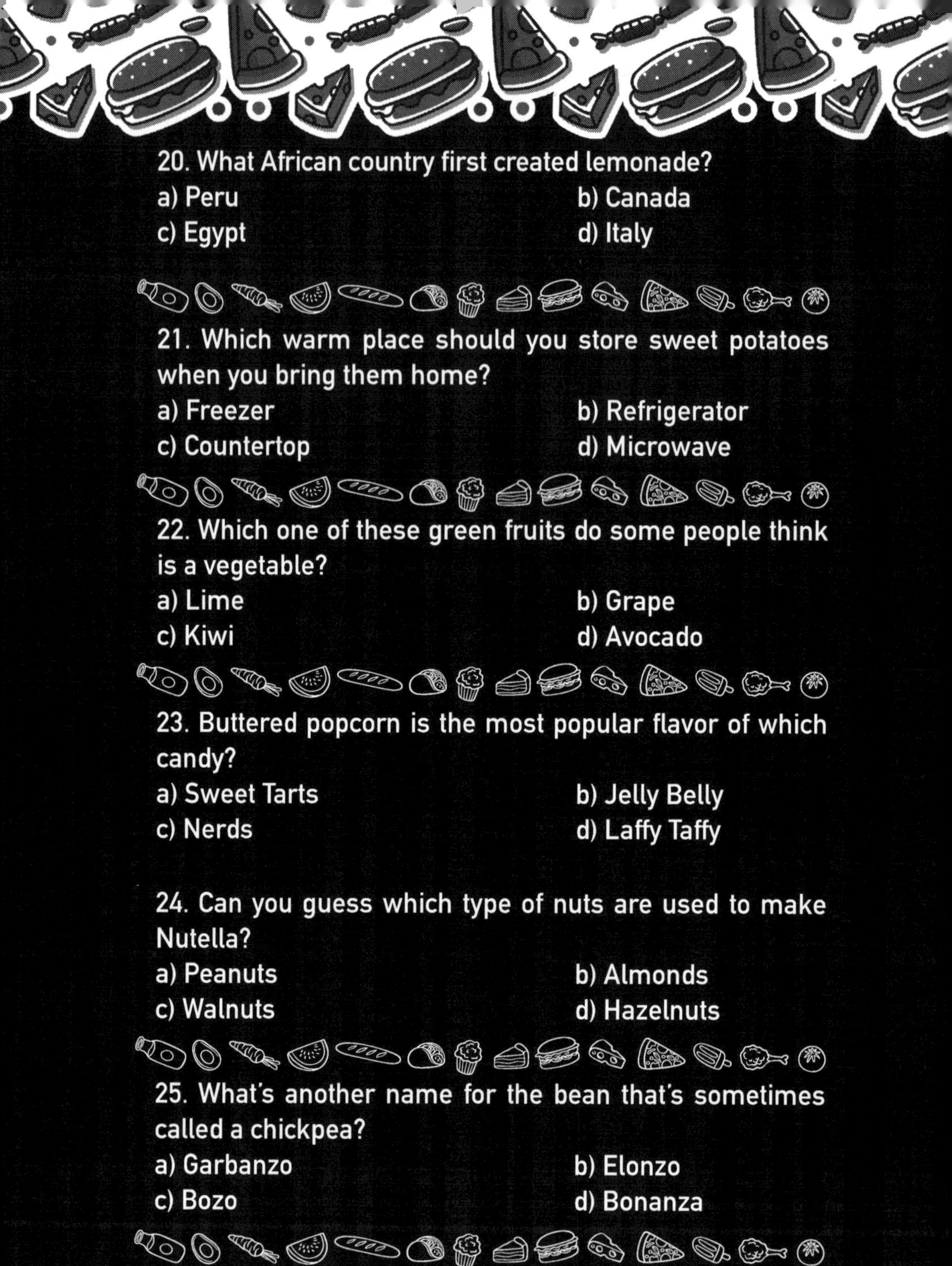

20. What African country first created lemonade?

a) Peru
b) Canada
c) Egypt
d) Italy

21. Which warm place should you store sweet potatoes when you bring them home?

a) Freezer
b) Refrigerator
c) Countertop
d) Microwave

22. Which one of these green fruits do some people think is a vegetable?

a) Lime
b) Grape
c) Kiwi
d) Avocado

23. Buttered popcorn is the most popular flavor of which candy?

a) Sweet Tarts
b) Jelly Belly
c) Nerds
d) Laffy Taffy

24. Can you guess which type of nuts are used to make Nutella?

a) Peanuts
b) Almonds
c) Walnuts
d) Hazelnuts

25. What's another name for the bean that's sometimes called a chickpea?

a) Garbanzo
b) Elonzo
c) Bozo
d) Bonanza

26. You should drink between five and 11 cups of what drink every day?

a) Milk
b) Soda
c) Water
d) Orange juice

27. What's the name of the curved-bottom pan used in a lot of Chinese cooking?

a) Skillet
b) Wok
c) Spatula
d) Dutch oven

28. Which one of these tiny berries freezes in just four minutes?

a) Banana
b) Blueberry
c) Kiwi
d) Lemon

29. What type of food is a banana?

a) Vegetable
b) Stone fruit
c) Berry
d) Meat

30. Which of these minerals sits in a shaker on most dinner tables?

a) Salt
b) Pepper
c) Butter
d) Garlic

ANSWER

1. b) McDonald's.
Since 1955, McDonald's has been an American favorite. The yellow glowing "M" outside of each restaurant is called the Golden Arches.

2. a) Root vegetables.
Vegetables like potatoes, carrots, and parsnips are sometimes called root vegetables. You are, in fact, eating the root of the plant.

3. c) Bangers and mash.
In the U.K., a mashed potato mountain topped with sausages is called bangers and mash. If you wanted bacon instead, it would be rashers and mash.

4. a) India.
Filled with all sorts of spices, Indian food has become popular all over the world. There are 22 different languages there, so each food might have a different name.

5. c) Elbow.
There are over 360 million boxes of mac and cheese sold every year, and most of them are made with elbow-shaped pasta.

6. d) Lamb.
Humans are called omnivores because they eat meat and plants, but vegans don't eat any animal products — not even butter. You certainly wouldn't find a vegan eating lamb.

7. a) Mustard.
On average, each person in the United States eats 70 hot dogs per year. There's a ton of toppings to choose from, but over 70% of people say mustard is their favorite.

8. b) Sushi.
Sushi was created in Japan, but it's loved all over the world. 62% of Americans love it, and Brazil eats more of it than any other country.

9. a) Peach.
Because of the big seed, or pit, in the middle, peaches belong to a family of fruits called stone fruits. Other stone fruits include plums, mangos, and cherries.

10. c) Sauerkraut.
Smelly and fermented, sauerkraut is made by layering shredded cabbage and salt. Sometimes, vinegar or sugar is added, but it's usually kept very simple.

11. a) Bagel.
Bagels might look like donuts, but they couldn't be more different. Aside from being more savory than donuts, bagels are baked and donuts are deep-fried.

12. c) Garlic.
It's just an old tale, but garlic is said to keep vampires away. Most of the world's garlic is grown in China and California.

13. b) Wendy's.
Since 1969, Wendy's has offered the Frosty as a dessert. If you look closely at the Wendy's logo, you'll see the word "Mom" at the bottom.

14. a) Ketchup.
Every June 5th, we celebrate Ketchup Day. Ketchup takes its name from a Chinese word for a fish sauce that may have started the ketchup trend.

15.c) Dill.
Most of the time, pickles are made using vinegar, salt, sugar, and dill. Dill is a weed that blooms with big white or yellow flowers.

16. d) Milkshake.
Since 1922, milkshakes have been an American favorite. They were invented in Chicago when a man named Pop started making them in his restaurant.

17. b) Mold.
Blue cheese is made with Penicillium mold cultures. It's the same mold that makes medicine you might get from your doctor for an infection.

18. d) Seed.
Chocolate starts life as a seed; then, it's processed into the sweet treat we love. During Mayan times, cacao seeds were used instead of money.

19. b) Pizza.
From New York to Beijing, there are over five billion pizzas ordered each year. Only 36% of people ask for pepperoni on it, though.

20. c) Egypt.
All the way back in 500 AD, Ancient Egyptians quenched their thirst with the first version of lemonade. Called qatarmizat, it was made with lemons and sugar like we make it today.

21. c) Countertop.
Many people think that sweet potatoes and yams are the same thing, but they are totally different. No matter which one you buy, it's best to store them on the countertop.

22 d) Avocado.
Avocados might not be sweet like other fruits, but it's not a vegetable. Avocados have more protein than any other fruit.

23. b) Jelly Belly.
Before buttered popcorn Jelly Belly jelly beans came along, Very Cherry was the favorite. Right now, there are over 50 different flavors of them on the shelves.

24. d) Hazelnuts.
Nutella is so popular that hazelnut farmers have had to start growing extra. Over 25% of all hazelnuts go to the Nutella factory.

25. a) Garbanzo.
Garbanzo beans, or chickpeas, first started to be farmed in 7500 BC. When they are planted, they leave the soil in better shape than it was before.

26. c) Water.
Depending on your age, you should drink at least five cups of water per day. About 60% of our bodies are made from water.

27. b) Wok.
Woks were created over 2,000 years ago! They are great for cooking because you can move the ingredients around to keep them from burning.

28. b) Blueberry.
On average, every person in the United States eats over a pound of blueberries every year. There are two types of them, but both types freeze really fast.

29. c) Berry.
It's crazy to think that a banana is a berry, but it is! Because all berries start with one flower, bananas couldn't be anything else.

30. a) Salt.
The human body holds as much salt as an entire box you would see on a store shelf. It was once used to pay Ancient Romans.

Chapter 8

GAMES AND TOYS

"Life is more fun if you play games"
~ Roald Dahl

Play along with these games and toy facts!

1. Can you guess which word game used to be called Criss-Cross Words?

a) Boggle
b) Sudoku
c) Scrabble
d) Go Fish

2. What's the name of the famous bricks that snap together to build almost anything?

a) Lego
b) Knex
c) Tots
d) Brickies

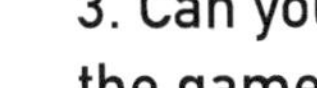

3. Can you put your left foot on red and guess the name of the game that was created in 1966?

a) Sorry!
b) Candyland
c) Twister
d) Boggle

4. You might dig with the help of a diamond pickaxe in which video game?

a) Fortnite
b) Rocket League
c) Minecraft
d) Lego Worlds

5. Do you know the name of the Nintendo character that first appeared in Donkey Kong?

a) Mario
b) Luigi
c) Bowser
d) Princess Peach

6. Which one of these games do you win when you land on the rainbow space?

a) Operation
b) Candy Land
c) Chutes & Ladders
d) Monopoly

7. What's the name of the board game with 100 squares and 10 snakes?

a) Chutes & Ladders
b) Jumanji
c) Connect Four
d) Checkers

8. Which one of these video games taught everyone how to floss?

a) Mario Kart
b) Fortnite
c) Plants vs. Zombies
d) Minecraft

9. Which one of these things would you never find in homemade slime?

a) Shaving cream
b) Glue
c) Glitter
d) Vinegar

10. Do you know which '80s doll was brought back as Cuties?

a) Cabbage Patch Dolls
b) Bratz
c) Barbie
d) Chatty Cathy

11. Can you guess the name of the talking '90s toy that you can connect to your smartphone now?

a) Teddy Ruxpin
b) Furby
c) Tamagotchi
d) Hatchimals

12. Can you name the card game that sees you asking your opponents for cards?

a) Uno
b) Solitaire
c) Rummy
d) Go Fish

13. You can be a thimble, a race car, or a shoe in which one of these classic games?

a) Risk
b) Chess
c) The Game of Life
d) Monopoly

14. What's the name of the toy that asks you to "pull it" and "twist it"?

a) Bop It
b) Push It
c) Tweak It
d) Pinch It

15. Do you know which one of these dolls comes all wrapped up in a ball?

a) LOL Surprise
b) American Doll
c) Bratz
d) Cabbage Patch Doll Cuties

16. If your opponent told you to "draw two" or changed the color, what game would you be playing?

a) Uno
b) Pinochle
c) Cribbage
d) Go Fish

17. What's the name of the tiny toy that attaches to one of your digits?

a) Tamagotchi
b) Fingerlings
c) Owleez
d) Bop It

18. What color does the eyes of an Owleez have to be before it will fly?

a) White
b) Red
c) Green
d) Pink

19. Can you guess which high-flying ball was made from a material called Zectron?

a) Wubble Ball
b) Bouncy Ball
c) Hoverball
d) Hippity Hop

20. What game has nine squares, o's, and x's?

a) Chess
b) Candy Land
c) Tic Tac Toe
d) Checkers

21. What's the name of the toy that's classified as a self-balancing scooter?

a) Hoverboard
b) Unicycle
c) Tricycle
d) Razor Crazy Cart

22. Which one of these toys would make your friends need to change into dry clothing?

a) Slinky
b) Super Soaker
c) Wubble Ball
d) Pogo Stick

23. Do you know which squishy toy sells more than 100 million cans every year?

a) Gak
b) Play-doh
c) Silly Putty
d) Kinetic Sand

24. What's the name of the toy you have to let break out of its shell?

a) Owleez
b) Furby
c) Hatchimals
d) LOL Surprise

25. You can draw lines with magnetic dust and knobs on which one of these toys' screens?

a) Etch-a-sketch
b) MagnaDoodle
c) Glow Board
d) Lite Brite

26. It has a ring you hold and a ball you bounce on; what's it called?

a) Bouncy Ball
b) Pogo Stick
c) Hippity Hop
d) Trampoline

27. Which game lets you perform surgery on a patient named Cavity Sam?

a) Operation
b) Hungry Hungry Hippos
c) Clue
d) The Sneaky, Snacky Squirrel Game

28. What's the name of the toy that can be made from metal or plastic but always walks down stairs?

a) Slinky
b) Chatter Phone
c) Mr. Potato Head
d) Kosmo

29. It takes a while to match the colors on all six sides of which toy?

a) Bop It
b) Rubik's Cube
c) Pyraminx
d) Jack-in-the-Box

30. What toy can light up plastic pegs with a light bulb placed in the back?

a) Lite Brite
b) Magna Doodle
c) Operation
d) Glow Worm

ANSWER

1. c) Scrabble.
Alfred Butts created Scrabble in 1933 because he wanted to cheer people up during The Great Depression. The name was changed in 1948.

2. a) Lego.
Since 1958, Lego bricks haven't changed at all. Every 2.8 seconds a set of Legos is sold around Christmastime.

3. c) Twister.
When Twister was created, it was almost called Pretzel. The name was already taken, but it's grown into one of the world's favorite party games anyway.

4. c) Minecraft.
You can play Minecraft in creative mode or in survival mode, and you can build nearly anything you want out of 3D blocks. It's been a big hit for Mojang since 2011.

5. b) Luigi.
If you want to see the original Mario, you would have to play Donkey Kong. Since then, he and his brother Luigi have tried to save the princess in many different games.

6. b) Candy Land.
If you can dodge the licorice spaces, it's easy to win Candy Land. It was created for polio patients in 1949.

7. a) Chutes & Ladders.
During a game of Chutes & Ladders, you'll spin the wheel almost 40 times. If you go first, you have a 1% higher chance of winning.

8.b) Fortnite.
Released in 2017, Fortnite has become a favorite and taught everyone how to dance. Moves like the Floss and The Robot are a great way to get some exercise.

9. d) Vinegar.
Slime was first put on the shelves in 1976, but it's a popular thing to make at home now. You would never find vinegar in the recipe because it's too acidic.

10. a) Cabbage Patch Dolls.
Xavier Roberts created Cabbage Patch Dolls in 1978, and they flew off of shelves. Later, they were brought back as smaller versions called Cuties.

11. b) Furby.
Resembling a small, furry owl, Furbys were all the rage when they came out. Now, Furby Connects are equipped with technology that makes them even more lifelike.

12. d) Go Fish.
Go Fish has roots in Ancient China, but the packaged version was created in 1984. Every game is played with exactly 52 playing cards.

13. d) Monopoly.
There have been over 250 million Monopoly games sold since 1933. There are now eight pieces you can choose to travel around the board — you could even be a battleship!

14. a) Bop It.
Created in San Francisco in 1993, Bop It has kept hands busy for a long time. If you wanted to break the world's record, you would have to beat the score of 1020.

15. a) LOL Surprise.
Part of the fun in getting a LOL Surprise doll is that you never know which one you'll get. Both Bratz dolls and LOL Surprise dolls were created by the same maker.

16. a) Uno.
The longest round in Uno history lasted for an amazing 170 hours! Shouting the word "Uno" when you have one card left is an idea that was taken from the game of Bingo.

17. b) Fingerlings.
Fingerlings are so cute and interactive, you'll never want to take them off your finger. Getting them wet destroys their technology, so you'll have to take them off to wash your hands.

18. a) White.
If you want your interactive Owleez to fly, you have to wait until its eyes turn white. Then, it will fly for 10 whole seconds!

19. b) Bouncy Ball.
Bouncy balls aren't like other balls. When they bounce for a second time, they go 98% higher than the first time they hit the ground.

20. c) Tic Tac Toe.
Using only a pencil and a grid with nine squares, Tic Tac Toe is easy to play anywhere. Are you good enough to get your x's or o's in a line before your opponent beats you?

21. a) Hoverboard.
Hoverboards can go on their own, but you still have to stay balanced. The average hoverboard can reach a speed of 8 miles per hour.

22. b) Super Soaker.
The Super Soaker was created when an inventor was trying to make a new kind of heat pump. They are so popular that over $1 billion dollars worth of them have been sold!

23. b) Play-doh.
Since it was created, the makers of Play-doh have mixed together over 700 million pounds. It sits next to the Furby and the Rubik's Cube on the best-selling toys list.

24. c) Hatchimals.
When you first get a Hatchimal, you need to wake it up with your hands. In about 45 minutes, you'll meet your new friend when it hatches out of an egg.

25.a) Etch-a-sketch.
Etch-a-sketch was created by a French Electrician sometime around 1950. These days, you can play with an Etch-a-sketch app on your parents' phone.

26. c) Hippity Hop.
Sometimes called a space hopper, the Hippity Hop is meant for kids only. If an adult who weighs too much tries to bounce on it, they'll pop the rubber ball!

27. a) Operation.
Operation was created back in the 1960s, but it takes its electronics from old fair games. Before they named it Operation, it was called Death Valley.

28.a) Slinky.
Slinkys work by transferring energy through their coils.
They also get to claim fame by being the official toy of Pennsylvania.

29. b) Rubik's Cube.
Rubik's Cubes take a minute to mess up and a lot of practice to get back together. Experts say that there are over 40 quintillion combinations of colors you can get by turning the pieces.

30. a) Lite
Brite. Lite Brite hasn't changed much at all since it was made in 1967. Back then, you could have bought one for under $7.00.

Chapter 9

Fictional Characters

"All our dreams can come true, if we have the courage to pursue them."
~ Walt Disney

They might not be real, but there's a lot to know about them

1. Can you remember how many fingers Mickey Mouse has on each hand?

a) 3
b) 5
c) 6
d) 4

2. Can you remember what Lightning McQueen's first name really is?

a) Woody
b) Martin
c) Montgomery
d) Bill

3. Which "Toy Story" character was named after the second man to walk on the moon?

a) Slinky Dog
b) Buzz Lightyear
c) Duke Kaboom
d) Wheezy

4. If Steve from Minecraft were real, how tall do you think he would be?

a) 23 feet tall
b) 6 feet tall
c) 144 feet tall
d) 200 feet tall

5. Can you remember the name of Peppa Pig's little brother?

a) George
b) Billy
c) Robert
d) Alex

6. What's the name of the van that Scooby Doo and crew ride around in?

a) The Crime Solver
b) Mystery Machine
c) Rolling Thunder
d) Ghost Wheels

7. Do you know the names of Harry Potter's mom and dad?

a) Leon and Karen
b) Bob and Jane
c) James and Lily
d) Andre and Linda

8. Do you know the name of the green emotion in the movie "Inside Out"?

a) Disgust
b) Sadness
c) Joy
d) Anger

9. Which one of these Sesame Street characters loves to take baths with a rubber duck?

a) Oscar the Grouch
b) Ernie
c) Big Bird
d) Elmo

10. What's the name of the young hero in the movie "Home Alone"?

a) Anthony
b) Lincoln
c) Michael
d) Kevin

11. Which Disney princess and her sister have the last name of Oldenburg?

a) Elsa
b) Tiana
c) Jasmine
d) Belle

12. The Pumpkin King is also which one of these beloved "The Nightmare Before Christmas" characters?

a) Victor van Dort
b) Oogie Boogie
c) Jack Skellington
d) Dr. Finkelstein

13. Do you know the name of Hermione Granger's first boyfriend?

a) Viktor Krum
b) Ron Weasley
c) Harry Potter
d) Draco Malfoy

14. Which one of these PBS characters lives in a clock that doesn't have hands?

a) Daniel Tiger
b) Arthur
c) Clifford
d) Sid

15. What western state do Angelica, Chuckie, and Tommy from "Rugrats" live in?

a) Hawaii
b) Florida
c) Texas
d) California

16. Which "Moana" character shares a name with one of the Hawaiian islands?

a) Heihei
b) Pua
c) Maui
d) Moana

17. When Beast Boy from "Teen Titans" changed color, what color did he become?

a) Red
b) Purple
c) Pink
d) Beige

18. Do you have any idea what Kermit the Frog's middle name might be?

a) Fred
b) The
c) William
d) David

19. What kind of weather led Santa to ask Rudolph to lead his sleigh team?

a) Hail
b) Heat wave
c) Rain
d) Fog

20. With her long tusks and stubby nose, what kind of animal is Pumbaa?

a) Lemur
b) Gazelle
c) Meerkat
d) Warthog

21. Can you remember the name of Dumbo's small best friend?

a) Timothy Q. Mouse
b) Billy Y. Mole
c) James P. Hamster
d) Randall R. Rat

22. Do you know the names of the super family from "The Incredibles?"

a) Marr
b) Parr
c) Barr
d) Larr

23. Nemo's dad is named Marlin; what's his mom's name?

a) Coral
b) Salty
c) Sandy
d) Shelly

24. Do you know the name of Gaston's sidekick in "Beauty and the Beast"?

a) Chip
b) Cogsworth
c) LeFou
d) Olaf

25. Do you know which one of these Disney ducks has his own day?

a) Huey
b) Dewey
c) Louie
d) Donald

26. What color are The Grinch's eyes now?

a) Yellow
b) Orange
c) Gray
d) Brown

27. Where did Ratatouille move to follow his dream of becoming a chef?

a) New York City
b) Paris
c) London
d) Los Angeles

28. Can you remember Boss Baby's real name?

a) Theodore Templeton
b) Richard Templeton
c) Martin Templeton
d) Alec Baldwin

29. Which one of these fruits do Minions love more than anything in the world?

a) Oranges
b) Plums
c) Bananas
d) Nectarines

30. Do you know what the "cinder" part of Cinderella's name means?

a) Queen
b) Ashes
c) Shoe
d) Pumpkin

ANSWER

1. d) 4.
Mickey Mouse has been around since 1928, and he's never had more than three fingers and one thumb on each hand.

2. c) Montgomery.
Before Lightning became a famous race car, he was called Montgomery. If he were a real car, he could go up to 200 mph!

3. b) Buzz Lightyear.
Buzz Lightyear's name was taken from Apollo 11 astronaut, Buzz Aldrin. He was enlisted to serve in Star Command on his home planet of Zurtron.

4. b) 6 feet tall.
Minecraft is more than a game! College professors teach classes about it, and they've figured out that a real-life Steve would be 6 feet and 2 inches tall.

5. a) George.
Peppa and her little brother George have been exploring the world together since 2004. There are only three actors who provide the voices for all the characters on the show.

6. b) Mystery Machine.
Scooby, Shaggy, Daphne, Velma, and Fred are always seen in the Mystery Machine, and Scooby takes up a lot of room. He is the Great Dane breed of dog.

7. c) James and Lily.
It must have come as a huge surprise to James and Lily Potter to learn that their son was so magical. They are soulmates bound by the patronus that wards of the evil of Dementors.

8. a) Disgust.
There are five emotions that keep Riley safe. Disgust is always there to make sure Jangles the Clown stays far away.

9. b) Ernie.
Bert and Ernie have been part of Sesame Street since 1969, when it first aired. Ernie is the one that's famous for his "Rubber Duckie" song, though.

10. d) Kevin.
When his parents forget to take him on a holiday trip, young Kevin is left to fend for himself. Many of his lines in the movie are made up on the spot.

11. a) Elsa.
Both Elsa and Anna from "Frozen" have the last name of Oldenburg. According to animators, Elsa has more hair than Rapunzel!

12. c) Jack Skellington.
To create Jack Skellington, over 400 different versions of his head were made. His ability to frighten people is the reason he became the Pumpkin King.

13. a) Viktor Krum.
Viktor Krum might have been Hermione's first boyfriend, but Ron Weasley was her first kiss. Her name comes from a play by William Shakespeare.

14. a) Daniel Tiger.
Daniel Tiger is a character who picks up where Mr. Rogers left off. He always wears a watch because his house doesn't tell time.

15. d) California.
Although the show never says what town the Rugrats live in, it does say that they live in California. It's one of the few cartoons that have a star on the Hollywood Walk of Fame.

16. c) Maui.
Maui is both the name of one of Hawaii's islands, and the name of a Hawaiian demigod. In the movie, Maui is a wrestler.

17. a) Red.
When Beast Boy visited Colony, genetic testing went all wrong. It turned his normally green skin to the color red, but he changed back later.

18. b) The.
You would have to read "The Kermit and Piggy" story to learn that Kermit's middle name is "the." No one really knows how old he is, though.

19. d) Fog.
Santa asked Rudolph to lead the sleigh on "one foggy Christmas Eve." Once he proved that his nose came in handy, he was always asked to play reindeer games.

20. d) Warthog.
Although Pumbaa from "The Lion King" is voiced by a male actor, she is a female warthog. Her best friend Timon is a meerkat.

21. a) Timothy Q. Mouse.
Since the original film came out in 1941, Timothy Q. Mouse has been Dumbo's best friend. Without him, Dumbo would have never had the confidence to fly.

22 b) Parr.
The super crime-fighting family from "The Incredibles" has the last name of Parr. Jack-Jack, Dash, and Violet call Helen and Bob their parents.

23. a) Coral.
Coral, Nemo, and Marlin are a family of clownfish. In the wild, a clownfish can lay up to 1,000 eggs at once, but Nemo and Marlin were only guarding 400 at the start of the film.

24. c) LeFou.
It's not that LeFou is necessarily a bad guy, it's that he loves Gaston so much he would do anything for him. In French, LeFou's name means "the fool."

25. d) Donald.
In human years, Donald Duck is now 86 years old! His very own Donald Duck Day is celebrated on June 9th.

26. a) Yellow.
When The Grinch was first created, his eyes were red. Since he appeared in the TV special "Halloween is Grinch Night," they have been yellowish-green.

27. b) Paris.
To learn from the best chefs, Ratatouille moves to Paris. If you pay attention, you'll notice that none of the humans in the film have toes.

28. a) Theodore Templeton.
Before becoming known as the CEO, Boss Baby, his name was Theodore Templeton. Alec Baldwin is the name of the actor who voiced the character.

29. c) Bananas.
No one knows why Minions love bananas so much, but it's funny to hear them say it. You don't hear them often, but each one of the Minions has a name.

30. b) Ashes.
Cinderella's name was taken from a word that means ashes. Her real name is Mary Beth Ella Gertrude; Cinderella is much easier to remember.

CHAPTER 10
FAMOUS PEOPLE IN HISTORY

"Never give up on what you really want to do.
The person with big dreams is more powerful than one with all the facts."
~ Albert Einstein

These people made history – can you remember them?

1. Which one of these classical composers wrote his first piece when he was only six?

a) Mozart
b) Chopin
c) Beethoven
d) Bach

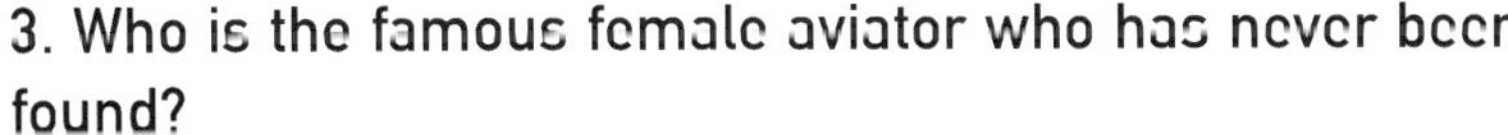

2. What's the name of the Civil Rights leader who's celebrated on January 18th?

a) Martin Luther King, Jr.
b) Abraham Lincoln
c) Mahatma Gandhi
d) Barack Obama

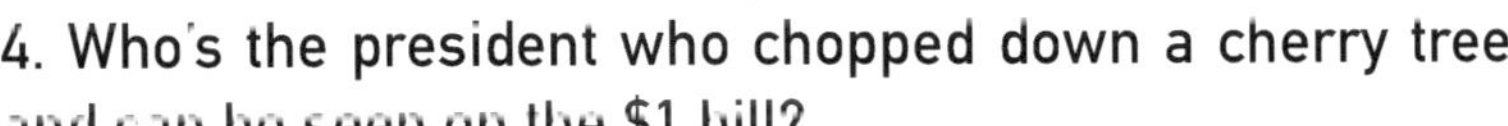

3. Who is the famous female aviator who has never been found?

a) Sally Ride
b) Amelia Earhart
c) Bessie Smith
d) Annie McClain

4. Who's the president who chopped down a cherry tree and can be seen on the $1 bill?

a) Bill Clinton
b) Benjamin Franklin
c) George Washington
d) Jimmy Carter

5. Which one of these things is Bill Gates partially responsible for creating?
a) Microsoft
b) iPad
c) Kindle
d) EchoDot

6. Which of these Civil Rights activists refused to give up her seat on an Alabama bus in 1955?
a) John Lewis
b) Rosa Parks
c) Martin Luther King, Jr.
d) Whitney Young

7. What's the name of the founding father who is rumored to have tied a key to a kite?
a) Benjamin Franklin
b) George Washington
c) John Hancock
d) Thomas Jefferson

8. Do you know which of these former presidents is often pictured wearing a top hat?
a) John Adams
b) Richard Nixon
c) Abraham Lincoln
d) Donald Trump

9. Can you remember the last name of the brothers who flew the first controlled plane?
a) Miller
b) Wright
c) Lopez
d) Lee

10. Do you know the names of the explorers that Pocahontas guided during an expedition?
a) Lewis and Clark
b) Van Gogh and Vasco de Gama
c) James Cook and
d) Ponce de Leon and

11. Can you name the blind and deaf woman who was the first severely disabled woman to graduate college?
a) Helen Keller
b) Florence Nightingale
c) Hedy Lamarr
d) Sojourner Truth

12. Do you know the name of the famous physicist who rarely combed his hair?

a) Steven Hawking
b) Marie Curie
c) Albert Einstein
d) Benjamin Franklin

13. What famous scientist used a special device to help him talk?

a) Stephen Hawking
b) Albert Einstein
c) Bill Nye
d) Thomas Edison

14. What's the name of the hearing-impared composer who wrote "Moonlight Sonata?"

a) Bach
b) Beethoven
c) Chopin
d) Wagner

15. What buggy band has members named George, Paul, Ringo, and John?

a) The Beatles
b) The Wasps
c) The Cockroaches
d) The Horseflies

16. What's the first name of the inventor, scientist, and artist named Da Vinci?

a) Raphael
b) Leonardo
c) Michelangelo
d) Roberto

17. What's the name of the astronaut who took "one giant leap for mankind' by walking on the moon?

a) Neil Armstrong
b) John Glenn
c) Jim Lovell
d) Buzz Aldrin

18. Can you name the beautiful Queen of Ancient Egypt who negotiated with the Romans?

a) Chloe
b) Catherine
c) Cleopatra
d) Cynthia

19. Who is the explorer whose name is often used as a pool game?

a) Marco Polo
b) Christopher Columbus
c) Vasco de Gama
d) Captain James Cook

20. What's the last name of the Dutch artist who lopped off his own ear?

a) Rembrandt
b) Picasso
c) Van Gogh
d) Warhole

21. Which one of these Roman leaders was kidnapped by pirates when he was young?

a) King Tut
b) Julius Caesar
c) Pope Francis
d) Brutus

22. What warm American state is former President Barack Obama from?

a) Hawaii
b) Rhode Island
c) Maine
d) South Dakota

23. Which of these scientists is said to have discovered gravity when an apple hit him on the head?

a) Isaac Newton
b) Albert Einstein
c) Eli Whitney
d) Alexander Graham Bell

24. Greta Thunberg is known across the world for her love of what?

a) Biscuits
b) Rare music
c) The environment
d) Textiles

25. Which of these bright things Thomas Edison famous for inventing?

a) Sparklers
b) Lightbulbs
c) Glow sticks
d) Lighthouses

26. What's the first name of the current and long standing Queen of England?

a) Meghan
b) Kate
c) Elizabeth
d) Sophie

27. Do you know the name of the artist who had one long eyebrow on her forehead?

a) Georgia O'Keeffe
b) Mary Cassatt
c) Yayoi Kusama
d) Frida Khalo

28. Who is the Nobel Peace Prize winning nun who later became a saint?

a) Mother Teresa
b) Mother Margaret
c) Mother Elizabeth
d) Mother Lydia

29. What did Ponce de Leon hope to find when he was exploring?

a) Gold
b) A fountain of youth
c) New kinds of flowers
d) Spices

30. What's the name of the girl who wrote about her life in hiding in a diary named Kitty?

a) Bridget Frank
b) Martha Frank
c) Anne Frank
d) Lisa Frank

ANSWER

1. a) Mozart.
Wolfgang Amadeus Mozart's dad knew he was talented, so he pushed him to write music. By the time he was 14, he had written an opera!

2. a) Martin Luther King, Jr.
During the 1960s, Martin Luther King, Jr. brought great attention to the Civil Rights Movement. You may have heard his "I have a dream" speech in one of your classes.

3. b) Amelia Earhart.
Before Amelia Earhart was a pilot, she was a nurse's aid. No one knows what happened to her plane in 1937, but people are still searching for clues.

4. c) George Washington.
A lot of people think George Washington had wooden teeth, but they were real. Before becoming the first president, he was a surveyor.

5. a) Microsoft.
Bill Gates runs a charity organization now, but he was only 32 when he started Microsoft. It's estimated that his IQ is over 150 — that makes him a genius!

6. b) Rosa Parks.
Rosa Parks was already an activist before she refused to move from her seat. Her actions led to the Montgomery Bus Boycott, a huge part of the Civil Rights Movement.

7. a) Benjamin Franklin.
If you were holding money with Benjamin Franklin's face on it, you would have a $100 bill. He is best-known for creating the lightning rod.

8. c) Abraham Lincoln.
The 16th President of the United States, Abraham Lincoln, mostly taught himself everything he knew. You'll often hear him called by his nickname, Honest Abe.

9. b) Wright.
When they were young, the Wright Brothers were fascinated with gliders. In 1902, they took flight themselves when they piloted their plane on Kitty Hawk, North Carolina's beach.

10. a) Lewis and Clark.
Lewis and Clark were assisted by Pocahontas. She knew how to communicate with fellow Native Americans, and her outdoor skills helped them survive a harsh winter.

11. a) Helen Keller.
Helen Keller was born without the ability to hear or see, but she never let it stop her. With the help of friends like Alexander Graham Bell, she went on to become a disabilities advocate.

12. c) Albert Einstein.
Even though Albert Einstein was a little eccentric, he was incredibly smart. Without him, we wouldn't have the theory of relativity.

13. a) Stephen Hawking.
Despite having Lou Gehrig's disease, Stephen Hawking became one of the world's most trusted physicists. He discovered that black holes emit radiation.

14. b) Beethoven.
Ludwig von Beethoven may have lost his hearing, but he still became one of the world's most respected composers. When he was young, he was sent to study Mozart.

15. a) The Beatles.
During the '60s, The Beatles took America by storm when they appeared on TV. Several of the band members are still playing music now.

16. b) Leonardo.
Leonardo Da Vinci was curious about everything! Even though he was so smart, he never went to school.

17. a) Neil Armstrong.
In 1969, Neil Armstrong became the first man to leave his spacesuit's footprint on the moon. His spacecraft was named Apollo 11.

18. c) Cleopatra.
When Cleopatra was queen in ancient times, her beauty was second to her intelligence. She successfully led her people through carefully thought out politics.

19. a) Marco Polo.
By the time Marco Polo was a teenager, he was already exploring the world. During the course of his life, he traveled over 15,000 miles.

20. c) Van Gogh.
Before painting famous pictures like "The Starry Night," Vincent Van Gogh was a member of the clergy. No one knows why he cut off his ear, but he painted over 900 paintings in his lifetime.

21. b) Julius Caesar.
Julius Caesar's birthday is July 13th. He passed away on the Ides of March, or as we call it, March 15th.

22. a) Hawaii.
Barack Obama was born on one of the Hawaiian islands. He rose through state leadership to become the first African American president to sit in the Oval Office.

23. a) Isaac Newton.
The story about Isaac Newton may or may not be true, but we wouldn't know the laws of gravity without him. His dog once knocked over a candle and burned down his lab.

24. c) The environment.
At only 17 years old, Greta Thunberg has been nominated for a Nobel Peace prize. Despite having Asperger's Syndrome, she always speaks up for the environment.

25. b) Lightbulbs.
Thomas Edison began experimenting in his own lab when he was only 10. He's most famous for inventing the lightbulb and the phonograph.

26. c) Elizabeth.
Queen Elizabeth II is quite down to earth for a royal. It's not uncommon to see her wear the same dress or to carry the same handbag more than once.

27. d) Frida Khalo.
Mexican artist Frida Khalo was in an accident when she was young. She spent most of her life wearing a cast around her ribcage, but she never let her injuries stop her.

28. a) Mother Teresa.
Mother Teresa committed her life to helping the less fortunate. By the age of 12, she knew exactly what she wanted to do with her life.

29. b) A fountain of youth.
Even though he looked for it, Ponce de Leon did not find the fountain of youth. He did discover Puerto Rico, though.

30. c) Anne Frank.
Anne Frank was given her diary, Kitty, when she was only 13 years old. Her sister Margot also kept a diary, but it has yet to be recovered.

Did you enjoy the book?

If you did, we are ecstatic. If not, please write your complaint to us and we will ensure we fix it.

If you're feeling generous, there is something important that you can help me with – tell other people that you enjoyed the book.

Ask a grown-up to write about it on Amazon. When they do, more people will find out about the book. It also lets Amazon know that we are making kids around the world laugh. Evena few words and ratings would go a long way.

If you have any ideas or jokes that you think are super funny, please let us know. We would love to hear from you. Our email address is -

riddleland@riddlelandforkids.com

https://pixelfy.me/riddlelandbonus

Thank you for buying this book. We would like to share a special bonus as a token of appreciation.
It is a collection of 50 original jokes, riddles, and two funny stories

Would you like your jokes and riddles to be featured in our next book?

We are having a contest to discover the cleverest and funniest boys and girls in the world !

1) **Creative and Challenging Riddles**
2) **Tickle Your Funny Bone Contest**

Parents, please email us your child's "original" riddle or joke. He or she could win a $25 Amazon gift card and be featured in our next book.

Here are the rules:

1) We're looking for super challenging riddles and extra funny jokes.

2) Jokes and riddles **MUST be 100% original** NOT something discovered on the internet.

3) You can submit both a joke and a riddle because they are two separate contests.

4) Don't get help from your parents UNLESS they're as funny as you are.

5) Winners will be announced via email or our Facebook group – Riddleland for kids.

6) In your entry, please con irm which book you purchased.

7) Email us at **Riddleland@riddlelandforkids.com**

Other Fun Books By Riddleland

Riddles Series

The Laugh Challenge Joke Series

Would You Rather Series

Get them on Amazon or our website at
www.riddlelandforkids.com

About Riddleland

Riddleland is a mum + dad run publishing company. We are passionate about creating fun and innovative books to help children develop their reading skills and fall in love with reading. If you have suggestions for us or want to work with us, shoot us an email at

riddleland@riddlelandforkids.com

Our family's favorite quote

"Creativity is an area in which younger people have a tremendous advantage since they have an endearing habit of always questioning past wisdom and authority."

- Bill Hewlett.

Made in the USA
Columbia, SC
11 December 2020